LOSING YOUR LUGGAGE

LOSING YOUR LUGGAGE

Finding Freedom from Sinful Baggage

A practical look at Romans 6–8

RICK REED

Heritage Seminary Press, Cambridge, Ontario
An imprint of H&E Publishing, Peterborough, Ontario, Canada

hesedandemet.com

© 2023 Heritage College & Seminary. All rights reserved. This book may not be reproduced, in whole or in part, without written permission from the publishers.

Scripture quotations are from the ESV® Bible (The Holy Bible, English Standard Version®), copyright © 2001 by Crossway, a publishing ministry of Good News Publishers. Used by permission. All rights reserved. The ESV text may not be quoted in any publication made available to the public by a Creative Commons license. The ESV may not be translated in whole or in part into any other language.

Editing and design by Janice Van Eck

Losing Your Luggage
Rick Reed
ISBN 978-1-77484-120-4 (paperback)
ISBN 978-1-77484-121-1 (eBook)

For Linda, my beloved travelling companion
on the journey to freedom.

Contents

Introduction	**Your journey toward freedom starts here!**	1
1	**Dying for freedom** | Romans 6:1–10	5
2	**Living your new identity** | Romans 6:11–14	11
3	**What freedom looks like** | Romans 6:15–23	19
4	**Why losing your luggage is so hard** | Romans 7:1–25	27
5	**No condemnation? No kidding!** | Romans 8:1–4	35
6	**Minding your mind** | Romans 8:5–8	45
7	**Physical spirituality** | Romans 8:9–17	53
8	**Groaning toward glory** | Romans 8:15–27	61
9	**Up to something good!** | Romans 8:28–30	69
10	**What you can never lose!** | Romans 8:31–39	77
	Conclusion | **Joy in the journey**	85
	Appendix 1 | **Your personal "Baggage Check"**	87

Introduction

Your journey toward freedom starts here!

Let me start you off with two true/false questions:

1. **When you became a Christian, your sins were forgiven.**
   True or false?
2. **When you became a Christian, you were freed from your sins.**
   True or false?

If you are like most people, you found the first one easier to answer than the second. You were able to answer "True" to the first question. You know the good news of the gospel declares all who become Christians are forgiven of their sins! As Romans 8:1 proclaims, "There is therefore now no condemnation for those who are in Christ Jesus."

But you may have found the second question a bit harder to answer. You were not so sure you could honestly say becoming a Christian frees a person from sin. When you look at your own life and the lives of other Christians, you don't see clear evidence of *freedom* from sin.

In fact, if you were candid, you'd have to admit to areas where you feel stuck in sin. Perhaps you struggle with an arrogant attitude that makes you come across as self-promoting, or it could be a critical spirit and a tendency to find fault with everyone around you. It might be a jealous heart which resents the good things others receive, or an explosive temper that erupts in ugly words. It could be a shadowy bondage to pornography. Or a deep-seated bigotry which looks down on people from some ethnic backgrounds. Maybe it's just a pervasive selfishness that keeps you from truly loving others.

If you struggled to answer "True" to the second question, if you carry some sinful baggage, I've got good news. *It's possible to lose your luggage and find freedom from the sins that weigh you down and hold you back!*

I say this because of the truth found in Romans 6–8. In these chapters we discover why we struggle to win over sin. We find out why we carry around so much sinful baggage. Best of all, we learn how to find freedom from the sins that enslave us.

Over thirty years ago, I had a seminary class where Dr. Bill Lawrence unpacked the truth of Romans 6–8 in a way I'd never seen before. It was liberating. It was life-giving. Over the past three decades, I've repeatedly come back to these chapters, digging deeper to understand and apply these crucial biblical concepts. I've also had the joy of teaching Romans 6–8 to others, helping them discover how to lose their sinful baggage and find greater freedom in Christ.

In *Losing Your Luggage*, I'll walk you through these three amazing chapters in Romans so you can see for yourself what God has to say. I want the truth of Romans 6–8 to impact you the way it has impacted me and countless other Christians who struggle with sin. As it does, you'll start to lose your sinful luggage and find a greater measure of freedom in Christ.

Getting the most out of this book

To gain maximum benefit from *Losing Your Luggage*, I'd ask you to complete the personal "Baggage Check" included at the back of this book (Appendix 1). The personal "Baggage Check" should only take you 10–15 minutes to complete. But I'm convinced it will be time well spent. Filling in the baggage checklist will clarify what luggage you most need to lose. It will help keep things real and practical.

Here's another travel tip. Read the following chapters with your Bible open. What I write in this book only matters if it lines up closely with God's Word. He's the One who tells us how to lose our sinful baggage and find our way to freedom.

Are you ready to begin a journey toward greater freedom in Christ? Ready to lose some luggage?

Let's get started!

Dying for freedom

Romans 6:1–10

Romans 6 begins with an important question for all of us who carry around sinful baggage: "What shall we say then? Are we to continue in sin that grace may abound?" (6:1).

The answer Paul gives to this question is both profound and perplexing: "By no means! How can we who died to sin still live in it?" (6:2).

Let that sink in: The Bible says Christians *died* to sin.

Paul's answer raises new questions: "If I died to sin, why is sin still so alive in me?" "Is Paul saying Christians won't struggle with sin anymore?" "Since sin seems alive and well in my life, does this mean I'm not really a Christian?"

We'll get answers to these important questions in due time, but first we need to understand why Paul says we died to sin. In verses 3–5, he lays down the theological basis for this astounding claim. Read these verses closely and follow his reasoning.

> ³ Do you not know that all of us who have been baptized into Christ Jesus were baptized into his death? ⁴ We were buried therefore with him by baptism into death, in order that, just as Christ was raised from the dead by the glory of the Father, we

too might walk in newness of life.
⁵ For if we have been united with him in a death like his, we shall certainly be united with him in a resurrection like his (6:3–5).

Do you see the reason Paul declares we died to sin? It all centres on your relationship with Jesus. When you link your life to Jesus through faith in him, God sees you as united with Jesus in his death (verse 3), burial (verse 4) and resurrection (verse 5). Since Jesus died to sin, you did too. Since Jesus was buried, you were too; this burial is pictured in your baptism. Since Jesus was raised to new life, you were too. In short, since Jesus died to sin and since you are united to Jesus, you died to sin.

I need to add that this is only true if you are a Christian. It's not enough to know about Jesus' death on the cross on Good Friday and resurrection from the grave on Easter Sunday. You must do more than believe it *historically*; you must receive it *personally*. You must link your life to Jesus through sincere faith in him. If you have, then what is true of Jesus is now true for you: you died to sin!

At this point, you may think, *This sounds great. But it also seems unrealistic. The Bible may say I died to sin, but sin sure doesn't seem dead to me! I'm still lugging around a lot of sinful baggage.*

Here's where we need to understand something very important about sin: sin has two sides. Sin has a seductive side and a slavery side. The seductive side of sin tempts us; the slavery side traps us. The seductive sin attracts us; the slavery side addicts us.

Think of the sins you struggle with most. I imagine you'd agree those sins have a seductive side. Sin markets itself quite well. It advertises itself in an attractive way. But, as you've undoubtedly found out, sin doesn't live up to its marketing promises. It may deliver short-term pleasure, but it always results in long-term pain. After enticing us, it enslaves us. Attraction turns to addiction. We no longer sin because we want to; pretty soon, we sin because we have to.

Now when Paul says we died to sin, do you think he's talking about the seductive side or the slavery side of sin? If you are unsure, look at verse 6 and you'll see the answer: "We know that our old self was crucified with him in order that the body of sin might be brought to nothing, so that we would no longer be enslaved to sin" (6:6).

Notice the final words in the verse: "so that we would no longer be enslaved to sin." The Bible teaches we died to the slavery side of sin. We haven't died to the seductive side of sin; Paul will make that painfully clear in chapter 7. But we have died to the slavery side. Since your life has become united with Christ through faith in him, God sees your "old self" as "crucified" with Christ. In Jesus, the penalty for your sins has been paid; you are now justified before God.[1]

Verse 6 says all this happened so the power of sin in your body might be "brought to nothing." As John Stott explains, sin has not become extinct, but it has been defeated; not annihilated, but deprived of power.[2] The end result is that your body no longer needs to remain "enslaved to sin."[3] If you are a Christian, you can confidently declare: "I died to the slavery side of sin."

The railroad to freedom

Some years ago, our family visited the National Underground Railroad Freedom Center in Cincinnati, Ohio. The museum sits on the banks of the Ohio River. That's significant because the river forms the boundary line between the states of Kentucky and Ohio.

---

[1] The Greek verb *dikaioo*, translated "set free from sin" in Romans 6:7, literally means to be "justified."
[2] John Stott, *Men Made New: An Exposition of Romans 6–8* (Grand Rapids: Baker, 1978), 44.
[3] As John Murray notes, "The body of the believer is no longer a body conditioned and controlled by sin. The body that is his now is one conditioned and controlled by what has come to be the ruling principle of the believer in his totality, namely, 'obedience unto righteousness' (vs. 16)." John Murray, *Epistle to the Romans* (Grand Rapids: Eerdmans, 1982), 221.

Back in the mid-nineteenth century, before Abraham Lincoln issued his Emancipation Proclamation, Kentucky was a slave state and Ohio was free. For that reason, many African American slaves risked their lives to cross the river and get to freedom. They often continued north on what was called the Underground Railroad, a network of secret routes and safe houses set up to help slaves escape to the northern United States or into Canada.

When our family toured the museum, we heard a plaintive, emotive Negro spiritual called "Oh Freedom." The lyrics to the song say,

> Oh, freedom!
> Oh, freedom!
> Oh, freedom over me!
> And before I'd be a slave
> I'll be buried in my grave
> And go home to my Lord and be free.[4]

Since slavery was so oppressive and dehumanizing, many risked their lives to find freedom. They would rather risk death than remain slaves.

If you have experienced an oppressive, dehumanizing enslavement to some area of sin, you have probably had moments when you've echoed the sentiment in this song. You say, "I'd rather die than stay enslaved to this temper of mine that explodes and drives people away." "I'd rather die than stay a slave to a sexual bondage that keeps me ashamed and in the shadows." "I'd rather die than remain trapped by a hard-driving, selfish ambition that ruins my relationships."

If you've felt that way, Romans 6 has good news for you. You have already died to the slavery side of sin. Old Slave Master Sin is no longer your slave master. You now belong to Christ.

---

[4] The background and lyrics of "Oh Freedom" can be found at https://balladofamerica.org/oh-freedom/; accessed December 16, 2021.

What we must know

According to Romans 6, your first step toward freedom as a Christian involves knowing this truth in a deeply personal way.[5] Notice how verse 6 begins with the words "We know." To find freedom you must take this truth to heart; you must know it to the core of your soul: You died to the slavery side of sin.

It's crucial to embrace the truth God's Word tells you about yourself. Here's why: Old Slave Master Sin will try to trick you into thinking you still belong to him. Sin wants to deceive you into thinking you remain trapped and in bondage.

Imagine yourself as one of the slaves who followed the Underground Railroad up to Canada to find freedom. One day, you spot your old slave-master and realize he has come looking for you. What's worse, he sees you and heads your way. With an angry, authoritative voice he shouts, "Where have you been? I've got work for you to do. Get back where you belong!"

Let me ask you: How much authority does your old slave master have over you now that you've made it safely to Canada? The answer is none. You've made it to freedom and no longer are a slave. However, on a practical level, the answer is: Your old slave master has as much authority over you as you give him. If you believe his lies about how you still belong to him, you will return to being a slave—even though you are now free.

The same principle holds true for you as a Christian. Your Old Slave Master Sin no longer has any authority over you. From Romans 6, you can know your life now belongs to Christ. God sees Jesus' death, burial and resurrection as your death to your old life and your resurrection to a new life. But unless you know this—really know it on a heart level—you will be tempted to revert to being a slave again to sin. Even though you died to the slavery side to sin.

---

5 The Greek verb *ginosko*, translated "know" in verse 6, often carries the idea of an experiential *heart* knowledge, not simply a cognitive *head* knowledge.

The first stop on your spiritual road to freedom begins at the cross and the empty tomb of Jesus. God wants you to know something monumental happened when you linked your life to Christ through faith in his death and resurrection. Whether your feel it or not, you have been set free from slavery to sin.

While there is still much more in Romans 6–8 you need to discover to live out your freedom from sin, the starting place is knowing what God says is true: You died to the slavery side of sin.

Once you personalize this amazing truth, you are ready to take the next steps toward losing your luggage. In the next chapter, you'll discover three life-changing steps you are now ready take on your journey to freedom!

Chapter 1 | Review

If you are a Christian (if you are "in Christ"), you died with Christ to sin.

You've died to the slavery side of sin not the seductive side of sin.

You no longer have to be "enslaved to sin." Freedom is possible!

The first step on the journey to freedom is knowing this truth.

Living your new identity

Romans 6:11–14

In the last chapter we learned a life-changing truth from the opening verses of Romans 6: If you are a Christian, you died to the slavery side of sin.

But since we still struggle with the baggage of habitual sins, this truth may seem both unlikely and unrealistic. You may wonder, *If that's true, why do I still find myself stuck in old ways of living?*

Let me tell you a story that might help you make sense of what's going on.

Over eighty years ago, in the city of Philadelphia, Pennsylvania, Douglas Rice was born. Normally, the birth of a baby brings joy and celebration. But not in this case. You see, Douglas was not born into a happy, healthy home. He never met his birth father. His mother was not able to care for him. So as an infant, Douglas was placed into an orphanage—Mother Keulher's Home for Boys.

From his earliest days, Douglas felt unwanted and unloved. The insecurity inside him bubbled up and erupted as anger. He acted out to get attention, to make people notice him. Douglas lived at Mother Keulher's until he was four years old. At the age of four, Douglas died. He was buried in a quiet ceremony in the heart of downtown Philadelphia.

I know Douglas' story because he told it to me. Many years later, when he was living in another city and going by another name, Douglas spoke to me about his life and death.

You probably have a few questions as you read this. Questions like: "How could Douglas tell his story if he died at the age of four?" We'll get to that in a few minutes.

First, let me pass along something else Douglas said. Something that has stuck with me for decades. It's a truth Douglas learned from studying Romans 6. A truth he had come to live out in a very personal way. A truth that dramatically changed his life. Here's what he said: "You can't live like you used to live, because you're not who you used to be."

We'll see the biblical basis for this statement as we continue our journey through Romans 6. And we'll discover how understanding and applying this truth helps you lose sinful baggage and move forward on your journey toward freedom.

In Romans 6:1–10, Paul explains a vital truth he wants us to know: All Christians have died to the slavery side of sin. But it's not enough to simply know this truth. We must do something with our knowledge. So, in verses 11–13, Paul highlights what we must do to make this truth come alive in daily life.

> ¹¹ So you also must consider yourselves dead to sin and alive to God in Christ Jesus.
>
> ¹² Let not sin therefore reign in your mortal body, to make you obey its passions. ¹³ Do not present your members to sin as instruments for unrighteousness, but present yourselves to God as those who have been brought from death to life, and your members to God as instruments for righteousness (6:11–13).

As you look closely at these verses, you'll discover three ways God wants you to respond.

Living your new identity

1. Consider it as true that you've been made new.

The first thing God commands you to do comes in verse 11: "So you also must consider yourselves dead to sin and alive to God in Christ Jesus." Here's an amazing fact about this verse: It's the very first command in the entire book of Romans. Paul has written 148 verses without giving us a single imperative. Up to this point in the book, his focus has been on what God has done for us in Christ Jesus. Now, Paul begins to detail what God wants us to do in response.

It's instructive to notice the first imperative Paul gives in Romans 6:11—the first thing he tells us to do—relates to our thinking. We are to "consider" ourselves dead to sin and alive to God in Christ Jesus. In other words, the Bible wants you to think differently about yourself. You are to count it as true that you've been made new.

The Greek word translated "consider" comes from the fields of mathematics and accounting.[1] It often carries the sense of adding things up, doing the math. In this case, you are to add up these facts:

> you died with Christ
> \+ you were buried with him
> \+ you were raised with Christ to new life

When you do the spiritual math and add it all up, you come to the conclusion given in verse 11: You have died to sin and are alive to God in Christ Jesus.

Don't miss this: Paul not only wants you to know this, he wants you to consciously consider it as true for your life. He wants this truth to shape the way you think and feel about yourself. Paul knows a change in your behaviour requires a change in your thinking. As

---

[1] *logizomai* in *A Greek-English Lexicon of the New Testament and Other Early Christian Literature*, 3rd ed., Logos online version.

John Stott reminds us, "The secret of holy living is in the mind."[2]

You may push back and say, "But I don't feel this to be true. Most of the time, I don't feel dead to sin or alive to God. It seems I'm being asked to engage in spiritual fiction, to believe things that aren't believable."

If that's your response, let me remind you of what we learned in the last chapter. Sin has two sides—a seductive side and a slavery side. Romans 6:1–10 announces we died to the slavery side. When we get to Romans 7, we'll learn we haven't yet died to the seductive side of sin. Sin till tempts us. So, counting yourself dead to sin doesn't require you to believe you are beyond being tempted. Rather, you count on the fact you no longer must remain trapped. You've been made a new person in Christ Jesus (2 Corinthians 5:17).

If you still find it difficult to count it as true that you've been made new, I want to remind you Paul doesn't say "feel" this is true. He says "consider" it true. He's calling you to change your thinking about yourself, regardless of how you feel about your situation. There is a spiritual logic here which transcends your current feelings.

In fact, if you don't change your thinking and consider it true that you've been made new, you will find it impossible to change your behaviour. We all act consistently with how we see the world and how we understand ourselves. The Bible is calling you to allow God's view of you to shape your view of yourself.

2. Refuse to loan your body to sin.

The second thing you are to do with the knowledge that you died to the slavery side of sin comes out in verses 12–13. These verses contain the next commands in the book of Romans.

> [12] Let not sin therefore reign in your mortal body, to make you obey its passions. [13] Do not present your members to sin as

---

[2] John Stott, *Men Made New* (Grand Rapids: Baker Book House, 1978), 50.

Living your new identity

instruments for unrighteousness, but present yourselves to God as those who have been brought from death to life, and your members to God as instruments for righteousness (6:12–13).

Notice how Paul refers to the parts of our bodies as "instruments." The Greek word Paul uses for instruments can refer to weapons or tools.[3] So, we are commanded not to let sin weaponize our bodies or use the parts of our bodies as tools.

If you go to some auto repair shops, you'll see a sign which says, "No tools loaned." Don't think about asking to borrow a socket wrench or screwdriver. They don't loan their tools to customers. Probably because they've learned the hard way that people can misuse or pilfer them.

In Romans 6:12–13, Paul says you need a "No tools loaned" policy when it comes to the parts of your body. After all, you've undoubtedly learned the hard way that sin misuses and abuses your body as a tool for doing wrong.

So, when sin tempts you to use your eyes to look at a sensual website, your mouth to speak harsh and hateful words, your ears to listen to some gossip, your feet to travel to a place of darkness, you need to say, "No tools loaned!" Because you are in Christ, your body belongs to God. It's now time to stop allowing sin to use parts of your body as its tools or weapons. Remember, you can't live like you used to live because you're not who you used to be.

3. Make yourself a present to God.

The last half of verse 13 explains the third thing you are to do as one who has been made new in Christ: "present yourselves to God as those who have been brought from death to life, and your members to God as instruments for righteousness." You are to present yourself to God.

---

[3] *hoplon* in *A Greek-English Lexicon of the New Testament and Other Early Christian Literature*, 3rd ed., Logos online version.

Notice the progression in verse 13. First, you present "yourself" to God; you give him your whole self—heart, mind, soul, body. Then, you get specific and present "your members to God as instruments for righteousness." Here you give God those parts of your body most prone to get used as tools for sinning. You pray, "Lord, I give you my eyes today; help me keep my eyes focused on what pleases you." Or, "Lord, here is my mouth; as I go through the day, help me speak honest and gracious words about others and to others." "Lord, I present my feet to you; keep me walking in your ways so I steer clear of people and places that pull me from you."

Making yourself a present to God lines up with what Paul writes later in Romans 12:1–2:

> [1] I appeal to you therefore, brothers, by the mercies of God, to present your bodies as a living sacrifice, holy and acceptable to God, which is your spiritual worship. [2] Do not be conformed to this world, but be transformed by the renewal of your mind, that by testing you may discern what is the will of God, what is good and acceptable and perfect.

As you reflect on what God's Word is saying in Romans 6 (and Romans 12), you will discover the way God changes our lives. First, he changes our *identity* by making us dead to sin and alive to God in Christ Jesus. Next, he works to change our *thinking* to match our new reality. We learn to view ourselves the way he does. Finally, he helps us change our *behaviour* to line up with our thinking. Over time—and it will take time—we begin to view ourselves as God does: dead to sin and alive to God. Gradually, we start to live out our new identity in Christ.

Back to Douglas Rice

That's what happened to Douglas Rice. I started to tell you Douglas' story at the beginning of this chapter. I imagine it seemed strange that Douglas could die at the age of four and later tell me the story of what happened. Let me fill in a few more important details to clear things up.

When Douglas was living at the orphanage, he was visited by William and Mildred Lawrence. The Lawrences invited Douglas to come to their home for short visits. After a while, they began the process of adopting him to be their son.

When Douglas was four, he went to the courthouse in downtown Philadelphia. A judge asked him if he wanted to live with the Lawrence family as their son. When he agreed, the adoption papers were signed and sealed. On that day, Douglas Rice legally died. They buried his original birth certificate in a file at the courthouse. From that day forward, he was given a new name: Bill Lawrence. No longer was he an orphaned child. He now had a new family and a new identity.

But, as Bill Lawrence explained, it took years before he began to live out his new identity. He still tended to see himself as unwanted and unloved. Anger still boiled up within him and spilled over to scald others. A sense of insecurity still shadowed him.

It took time before his new identity began to really sink in. But slowly it did. More and more he realized he was no longer Douglas Rice. He was now Bill Lawrence—a person with a new identity and a loving family. As his thinking about himself began to line up with his new identity, he saw positive changes in his attitudes and actions. He still had an outgoing personality, but the anger and insecurity subsided. He began to live more and more as Bill Lawrence and less and less like Douglas Rice.

One day, while studying Romans 6, he realized he was a living illustration of the spiritual truth Paul presents. As a child in the orphanage, he had died and legally become a new person. As a child of God, he had died to sin and become a new person in Christ. As he came to understand and embrace this new identity, he saw positive changes take place in his life. Bill came to understand the message of Romans 6: *You can't live like you used to live because you're not who you used to be.*

The same will be true for you. As you come to understand and embrace the new identity you have in Christ—dead to sin and alive to God—you'll begin to live differently. The truth of Romans 6 will begin to change the way you think and live. Remember: *You can't live like you used to live because you're not who you used to be.*

In Christ, you've been set free to live out your new identity. But what will this look like in daily life? The answer to that question may surprise you. I'll explain in the next chapter.

Chapter 2 | Review

In Christ, you have a new identity:
you are dead to sin and alive to God.

———

You can't live like you used to live because
you are not who you used to be.

———

Consider it true that you have been made new
(even if you don't feel new).

———

Refuse to loan your body to sin.

———

Make yourself a present to God.

———

What freedom looks like

Romans 6:15–23

I've never been a big Bob Dylan fan. Maybe that's because I was too young back in 60s when his songs moved a whole generation. Maybe it's because I never could develop a taste for his voice; his singing always sounded more like moaning than music to me. But though I've never been a Bob Dylan fan, I have a favourite Bob Dylan song. It's a track from his *Slow Train Coming* album called "Gotta Serve Somebody."[1]

The title of the song sums up the main message: everyone—regardless of who you are—has to serve somebody. As Bob sings it, you may be an ambassador, a bus driver, a TV network executive, a preacher or drug dealer but the truth remains the same:

But you're gonna have to serve somebody, yes indeed
You're gonna have to serve somebody
Well, it may be the devil or it may be the Lord
But you're gonna have to serve somebody.

---

[1] Bob Dylan, "Gotta Serve Somebody," *Slow Train Coming* (New York: CBS Records, 1979).

I don't know if Bob Dylan ever read Romans 6, but the punch line of his song sure sounds like it. In fact, the last line of "Gotta Serve Somebody" paraphrases what the Bible says in Romans 6:16: "You are slaves of the one whom you obey, either of sin, which leads to death, or of obedience, which leads to righteousness."

Long before Bob Dylan made music, the apostle Paul made it clear that every person will serve somebody—either sin or obedience, either the devil or the Lord.

You may object to Paul's language of being a slave to sin or obedience. After all, we live in a land of freedom. We abolished slavery years ago. Each of us enjoys the freedom to live as we see fit.

If you object to the binary choice of serving either the devil or the Lord, you're not alone. The religious leaders in Jesus' day had the same reaction. They claimed to be nobody's slave: "We are offspring of Abraham and have never been enslaved to anyone" (John 8:33). Jesus reminded them that even religious people can find themselves in spiritual bondage: "Truly, truly, I say to you, everyone who practices sin is a slave to sin" (John 8:34).

If we are honest with ourselves, we know Jesus speaks truth when he talks about being slaves to sin. We all know what it's like to live in bondage to destructive behaviours or damaging habits and patterns. It might be anger, worry or jealousy, pornography or pride; the list goes on.

God knows all about our sinful baggage and spiritual bondage. In Romans 6–8, he tells us how we can lose our luggage and find our way to freedom. He even explains what true freedom looks like. And here's the surprise: *Freedom from sin looks like slavery to God.*

Take a close look at what Paul writes in Romans 6:15–23:

15 What then? Are we to sin because we are not under law but under grace? By no means! 16 Do you not know that if you present yourselves to anyone as obedient slaves, you are slaves of the one whom you obey, either of sin, which leads to death, or of obedience, which leads to righteousness? 17 But

thanks be to God, that you who were once slaves of sin have become obedient from the heart to the standard of teaching to which you were committed, [18] and, having been set free from sin, have become slaves of righteousness. [19] I am speaking in human terms, because of your natural limitations. For just as you once presented your members as slaves to impurity and to lawlessness leading to more lawlessness, so now present your members as slaves to righteousness leading to sanctification.

[20] For when you were slaves of sin, you were free in regard to righteousness. [21] But what fruit were you getting at that time from the things of which you are now ashamed? For the end of those things is death. [22] But now that you have been set free from sin and have become slaves of God, the fruit you get leads to sanctification and its end, eternal life. [22] For the wages of sin is death, but the free gift of God is eternal life in Christ Jesus our Lord.

In these verses Paul essentially says, "You gotta serve somebody." Each of us will either be a slave to sin or a slave to God. Let's take the options one at a time.

Slavery to sin (aka bondage)

Some people think, *Well, if my choice is to serve sin or to serve God, I'll take my chances with sin. I don't want to give up some things I enjoy just because the Bible calls them sinful.*

Paul answers with a painful reminder: Sin is a harsh master. In fact, Paul lays out three reasons why serving sin is a lousy option.

1. Sin gets addictive.

Notice the words Paul uses to talk about sin in verse 19: lawlessness leading to more lawlessness." Sin never stays static; it always increases. It has a repetitive quality that becomes habit forming and addictive. You think you can control it, but it always ends up controlling you.

2. Sin brings shame.

In verse 21, Paul categorizes past sins as "the things of which you are now ashamed." Who doesn't have a few shameful memories of past sins? I remember a high school friend who turned his life over to Christ after realizing sin was getting the best of him and bringing out the worst in him. He came home from a party so drunk he couldn't remember what had happened. When his friends jokingly reminded him of what he had done at the party, he was so ashamed he realized it was time for a change. The fun evaporated; the shame remained.

3. Sin leads to death.

Three times in verses 15–23, Paul links sin to death (vv. 16, 21, 23). Let that sink in. Sin and death are business partners. They work out of different offices, but they team up to destroy us and damage those we love.

Consider the destruction caused by pornography. It's far from a private pleasure that doesn't hurt anyone. If you doubt that, talk to folks who run sexual recovery programs. They will tell you their clients regularly report increased rates of marital and mental health problems. One recovery program found 70 per cent of those addicted to pornography had contemplated suicide.

When it comes to the destruction caused by sin, it's not just the obvious or egregious sins that cause problems. Even "respectable" sins like pride, bitterness or envy will poison our souls, rob us of vitality and joy and kill our relationships with others.[2] No wonder Paul reminds us, "The wages of sin is death" (6:23).

Romans 6 rips the appealing façade off sin by showing how it addicts, shames and destroys. Sin is always a harsh master. That's why the message of our liberation from slavery to sin comes as such welcome news. The first half of Romans 6 announces liberating news: In Christ, we have died to the slavery side of sin. Now, in the

---

[2] See Jerry Bridges, *Respectable Sins* (Colorado Springs: NavPress, 2017).

last half of the chapter, we learn some surprising news: Freedom in Christ means slavery to God.

Slavery to God (aka freedom)

Paul makes it unmistakably clear that all who have been set free from slavery to sin have become "slaves of righteousness" (v. 18) and "slaves of God" (v. 22). Here's the paradox of Christian freedom—it is found by becoming slaves to God.

Paul readers knew all about slavery. Estimates put the number of slaves in the Roman empire at 10 to 20 per cent of the population.[3] Some slaves undoubtedly had malicious, oppressive masters (1 Peter 2:18). No wonder Paul encouraged slaves to gain their freedom if possible (1 Corinthians 7:21).[4]

Despite its limitations, Paul chose to use the imagery of slavery to make several important points. Let me highlight two important implications coming from the slavery to God analogy found in verses 15–23.

1. Slavery to God is true freedom.

Most people would say freedom involves following your heart, living out your deepest desires. In a sense, Paul affirms this understanding of freedom when he writes,

> [17] But thanks be to God, that you who were once slaves of sin have become obedient from the heart to the standard of teaching to which you were committed, [18] and, having been set free from sin, have become slaves of righteousness (6:17–18).

---

[3] British Museum. https://www.britishmuseum.org/exhibitions/nero-man-behind-myth/slavery-ancient-rome#:~:text=Scholars%20estimate%20about%2010%25%20(but,and%20ten%20million%20were%20enslaved; accessed January 31, 2022.
[4] For a helpful discussion of the Bible's perspective on slavery, see Rebecca McLaughlin, *Confronting Christianity* (Wheaton: Crossway, 2019).

Notice how Paul says those who were once slaves to sin have had a change of heart; they had "become obedient from the heart." Their deepest desires were now aligned with God's will. They freely chose to be "slaves of righteousness."[5]

In the Old Testament, we read of slaves who had such love and high regard for their masters that they voluntarily chose to remain bondslaves instead of being released. Moses describes this scenario:

> [16] But if he says to you, "I will not go out from you," because he loves you and your household, since he is well-off with you, [17] then you shall take an awl, and put it through his ear into the door, and he shall be your slave forever. And to your female slave you shall do the same (Deuteronomy 15:16–17).

Christians know God as a merciful and gracious Master. He has redeemed us from slavery to sin and given us new life in Christ (6:6–11). Out of grateful hearts, we choose to obey him from our hearts. What could be called slavery actually frees us up to live a new life in Christ.

2. Slavery to God is ultimate fulfilment.

Paul is not finished with the imagery of slavery. He uses it to make another important point related to benefits and outcomes. He declares that all who remain slaves to sin produce poisonous fruit: "But what fruit were you getting at that time from the things of which you are now ashamed?" (6:21). Even worse, slavery to sin pays painful wages: "For the wages of sin is death" (6:23).

On the other hand, slavery to God gives you the best of all outcomes: "But now that you have been set free from sin and have become slaves of God, the fruit you get leads to sanctification and

---

5 As Douglas Moo states, "Christian freedom is at the same time a kind of 'slavery.' Being bound to God and his will enables the person to become 'free'—to be what God wants that person to be." Douglas Moo, *The Letter to the Romans*, The New International Commentary on the New Testament (Grand Rapids: Eerdmans, 2018), 428.

its end, eternal life" (6:22). Sin earns death for all who choose to remain its slaves. God freely gives eternal life for those who are in Christ: "For the wages of sin is death, but the free gift of God is eternal life in Christ Jesus our Lord" (6:23).

Charles Spurgeon sums it up better than Bob Dylan:

> Every man must serve somebody: we have no choice as to that fact. Those who have no master are slaves to themselves. Depend on it, you will either serve Satan or Christ, either self of the Saviour. You will find sin, self, Satan, and the world to be hard masters; but if you wear the livery of Christ, you will find him so meek and lowly of heart that you will find rest unto your souls.[6]

As we come to the end of Romans 6, you may be eager to apply what you've learned so you can shed some sinful baggage. Out of love for Christ, you may be ready to obey him and experience true freedom. But I've got some bad news for you. There's still a problem. One you must face to lose your luggage. We'll discover this problem in our next chapter.

---

[6] Quoted in Michael Reeves, *Rejoicing in Christ* (Downers Grove: Inter-Varsity Press, 2015), 88.

Chapter 3 | Review

"You gotta serve somebody." You will either be a slave to sin or to God (Romans 6:22)

―――――

Sin is a harsh master—it's addictive, shameful and deadly.

―――――

As strange as it sounds, true freedom is found in slavery to God.

―――――

Freedom in Christ brings ultimate fulfilment from God.

―――――

Why losing your luggage is so hard

Romans 7:1–25

Did you know it's very possible to be sincerely frustrated as a Christian? To be both sincere and frustrated at the same time? Did you know it's possible to count yourself dead to sin and still find sin very much alive in you? Did you know it's possible to try your hardest as a Christian and yet still fall flat as a Christian?

I know this can happen because I've lived this story. And I've spoken to others who have too. More importantly, I know it's possible because Romans 7 follows Romans 6. I realize I sound like Captain Obvious to say Romans 7 follows Romans 6, but this is actually a very important observation.

You see, after working your way through Romans 6, you could conclude you are good to go when it comes to winning the battle with sin. After all, Romans 6 announces some incredibly good news. You've died to the slavery side of sin (6:6). You can count yourself dead to sin and alive to God in Christ Jesus (6:11). You've been set free from sin and have become a slave of righteousness (6:18, 22). You don't have to live like you used to live because you're not who you used to be!

But then you hit Romans 7.

Romans 7 pours cold water on the fires of spiritual passion ignited by Romans 6. Romans 6 is sunshine and blue skies; Romans 7 is overcast and stormy weather. If Romans 6 promises liberation, Romans 7 shouts frustration.

In Romans 7, Paul makes a powerful but painful point: Finding freedom from the sins that trip you up and pull you down takes more than what you learned in Romans 6.

So, let's take a closer look at the sobering spiritual news explained in Romans 7. I suspect you will find this chapter both depressing and comforting. Depressing because it dashes your hopes for easy spiritual victories. Comforting, because it lets you know that the struggle you live with is not unique to you. The apostle Paul had the same experience.[1]

Fleshing out our problem

Paul's focus in the first half of Romans 7 centres on the "the place of the law in Christian discipleship, now that Christ has come and inaugurated the new era."[2] He emphatically refutes the charge that our struggle with sin points to a deficiency in God's Law. The problem is not with God's Law but with us—the lawbreakers. Read how Paul explains it in Romans 7:14–20:

> [14] For we know that the law is spiritual, but I am of the flesh, sold under sin. [15] For I do not understand my own actions. For I do not do what I want, but I do the very thing I hate. [16] Now if I do

---

[1] I understand Paul to be speaking of his spiritual struggle as a Christian in Romans 7:14–25. Some biblical scholars interpret these verses differently, claiming Paul is looking back at his pre-Christian self or describing the experience of all who seek to keep God's Law. For a helpful summary of the arguments for each position see *Perspectives On Our Struggle with Sin: Three Views of Romans 7*, ed. Terry Wilder (Nashville: B&H Publishing, 2011).

[2] As John Stott observes, "The 'law' or the 'commandment' or the 'written code' is mentioned in every one of the chapter's first fourteen verses, and some thirty-five times in the whole passage which runs from 7:1 to 8:4." John R. Stott, *The Message of Romans* (Downers Grove: Inter-Varsity Press, 1994), 189.

what I do not want, I agree with the law, that it is good. ¹⁷ So now it is no longer I who do it, but sin that dwells within me. ¹⁸ For I know that nothing good dwells in me, that is, in my flesh. For I have the desire to do what is right, but not the ability to carry it out. ¹⁹ For I do not do the good I want, but the evil I do not want is what I keep on doing. ²⁰ Now if I do what I do not want, it is no longer I who do it, but sin that dwells within me.

Can you sense the frustration in Paul's heart? He's clearly conflicted, a battle rages inside him. The things he wants to do, he doesn't do. The things he wants to avoid, he does.

If you asked Paul why it's still so hard to find freedom from the sins which shadow us, his answer in Romans 7 would be two words: *the flesh*.

Paul's answer raises several important questions: What exactly is the flesh? How does it weaken our efforts to obey God and keep his commands? As we reflect on what Paul writes in Romans 7, we learn three important truths about the flesh.

1. The flesh is part of you, but not the heart of you.

Notice in verse 18 how Paul indicates the flesh is part of us, but not all of us. "For I know that nothing good dwells in me, that is, in my flesh." Paul is careful to qualify his declaration that nothing good dwells in him by adding the phrase, "that is, in my flesh." In other words, the flesh is part of him, but not all of him. In fact, it's not the deepest part of him. Look what he says in the last half of verse 18: "For I have the desire to do what is right, but not the ability to carry it out." Paul affirms he desires to please God. That's the deepest part of him.

Here's the first thing you need to know about the flesh: It's part of you, but not the heart of you. As a Christian, you have a new heart. When you trusted in Jesus, God gave you a new heart. He removed your heart of stone and replaced it with a new, living one. This is a central part of the New Covenant promise made by Ezekiel: "And

I will give you a new heart, and a new spirit I will put within you" (Ezekiel 36:26; see also Jeremiah 31:31–34).

In Christ, you've become a new person with a new heart. Now, the deepest part of you wants to please God. (By the way, one piece of evidence that you are truly a Christian is the presence of a new desire to please the Lord, a longing to turn from sin and walk in his ways.) The deepest and truest part of you has become a "new creation" (2 Corinthians 5:17).

So, the first thing you need to know about the flesh is that it's part of you, but not the heart of you. Let's move to the second thing.

2. The flesh is the leftover mindset and muscle memory from your old life.

You may be thinking, *So the flesh is part of me but not the heart of me. Exactly what part of me is it?* Romans 7 (and 8) give you an answer to this question. The Bible tells us the flesh refers to the leftovers from your old life before you were "in Christ." Specifically, these leftovers include both a sinful mindset (your thoughts) and some sinful muscle memory (your actions). Let's consider them one at a time.

(a) Mindset

The flesh includes a mindset slanted away from God and toward sin. Paul goes on to describe this sinful mindset in Romans 8:5–8:

> ⁵ For those who live according to the flesh set their minds on the things of the flesh, but those who live according to the Spirit set their minds on the things of the Spirit. ⁶ For to set the mind on the flesh is death, but to set the mind on the Spirit is life and peace. ⁷ For the mind that is set on the flesh is hostile to God, for it does not submit to God's law; indeed, it cannot. ⁸ Those who are in the flesh cannot please God.

Notice the link between the flesh and a sinful mindset. The mind set on the flesh sees sin as appealing and righteousness as repugnant.

Every one of us was born "in the flesh" (7:5) with a fleshly mindset. Our default way of thinking orients us toward ourselves and draws us toward sin. Our natural outlook "has at its center our fallen human perspective, which displaces God and his truth from the world, and which makes sin look normal and righteousness seem strange."[3]

So even if you became a Christian at a young age, even if you've always been a basically "good" person, you still were born with a mindset that instinctively revolves around self and gravitates toward sin. As Paul explained back in Romans 5, all of us were born as sons and daughters of Adam. We inherited a spiritual DNA that is fleshly. As Dave Roper puts it, we all were thrown into the world as a curveball, and the break is always down and away—down toward sin and away from God.[4]

When you became a Christian, you received a new heart, but you carried forward some old ways of thinking, many of which are unconscious.[5] No wonder the Bible calls us to "be transformed by the renewal of your mind" (Romans 12:2). Even as new creations, we easily think in old patterns. It takes time to develop a renewed mind.

If you are married, you know on your wedding day your identity changed. You joined your life to another person in a deep, lasting way. You were now singing a duet, not a solo. But you still had to learn to adjust your thinking to your new reality. You had to stop thinking "me" and start thinking "we." It took time to take on a married mindset.

The same thing holds true when you link your life to Jesus by faith. In a moment, your identity changes. Instead of being "in Adam" you are now "in Christ." Instead of being enslaved to sin, you now

---

[3] David Wells, *Losing Our Virtue: Why the Church Must Recover Its Moral Vision* (Grand Rapids: Eerdmans, 1999), 4.
[4] David Roper, *Psalm 23: The Song of a Passionate Heart* (Grand Rapids: Discovery House Publishers, 1994), 78.
[5] Charles Hodge explains: "Sin...is presented as an abiding state of the mind, a disposition or principle, manifesting itself in acts." Charles Hodge, *Commentary on the Epistle to the Romans* (Grand Rapids: Eerdmans, 1980), 232.

belong "to another, to him who has been raised from the dead" (7:4). But you still carry forward some old patterns of thinking into your new life in Christ. The leftovers from your self-oriented, sinful mindset constitute part of what Paul labels "the flesh."

(b) Muscle memory

"The flesh" also refers to sinful muscle memory. It's instructive that Paul speaks of sin "dwelling" in his physical body: "sin that dwells in my members" (7:23). Paul doesn't mean our bodies are innately sinful; rather, he is saying sin still has a hold on our bodies.

I find it helpful to think of the flesh as a kind of a spiritual muscle memory. By muscle memory, I'm referring to the procedural memory in our brains which allows us to do certain tasks without conscious thought. Take riding a bike. If you've learned to ride a bike, your body remembers how it's done, even if you don't get on a bicycle for a long time. That's muscle memory.

The flesh has a kind of spiritual muscle memory which makes sinning effortless. Your brain develops a procedural memory that kicks in and makes it easy to sin. Like riding a bike. Way too easy!

But there's a third thing you need to know about the flesh. And this is the worst news of all.

3. The flesh remains stronger than your good intentions and best efforts.

Did you notice how Paul talks about wanting to do the right thing but still finding himself doing the wrong thing? "For I do not understand my own actions. For I do not do what I want, but I do the very thing I hate" (7:15). He's got the right desires but can't carry them out. His intentions are good and his effort is commendable. But he keeps failing and falling.

Paul admits the flesh is stronger than his good intentions and best efforts. Let that sink in. This is the apostle Paul. A man who seems to us as godly and committed as they come. If Paul can't do it, what chance do you and I have?

Why losing your luggage is so hard

Some years ago, I watched a TV show called *The World's Strongest Man* where incredibly muscular men competed for the title of "World's Strongest Man." To win the crown, they had to lift ridiculously heavy objects. For one part of the competition, they put on a harness attached to a large, plexiglass container filled with coins. Their task was to lift the container off the ground.

I remember watching one burly guy give it a go. With swagger and confidence, he put on the harness and gave it all he had—groaning and grunting as he tried to lift the container. Despite his determined efforts, he couldn't budge it. Ultimately, he gave up.

Just imagine you were in the crowd watching the competition. Suppose the TV announcer offered you a chance to put on the harness and try to lift the container. Would you give it a go? Would you think you had a chance to succeed where the weightlifter failed?

Of course not. You'd be thinking, *If that guy couldn't lift the load, there's no way I can.*

Here's my point. We rightfully consider the apostle Paul a heavyweight Christian. His level of spiritual dedication and determination exceeded anything we've known or shown. But when it came to carrying out God's law, Paul says he couldn't do it. And if he fell short, so will you.

Business author Peter Drucker famously said, "Culture eats strategy for breakfast." He means no matter how good a company's business strategy may be, the culture of the organization has a much stronger impact on its efforts to succeed. We could paraphrase Paul's teaching in Romans 7 by saying, "The flesh eats good intentions for breakfast." No matter how sincerely you try to obey the Lord and keep clear of sin, the flesh will still overcome your good intentions.

Is this making sense? Are you getting the picture as to why you still struggle with sin? Is it sinking in that, even though you are a new person in Christ, you still battle old patterns of thinking and acting? Finding freedom is still hard because of the potency of the flesh.

No wonder we hear Paul cry out in frustration, "Wretched man that I am! Who will deliver me from this body of death?" (7:24).

If you are a sincerely frustrated Christian, you have echoed those words more than once!

A glimmer of hope

Romans 7 discourages and dashes the illusion that you can find freedom from sin through simply understanding your new identity in Christ and giving obedience your best efforts. But Romans 7 doesn't leave you in complete despair. The chapter concludes with a glimmer of hope. Paul answers his own question by pointing to Christ: "Thanks be to God through Jesus Christ our Lord!" (7:25).

Praise God, Jesus has made a way for us to break the sin cycle and find freedom. If you are tired of getting pinned by sin, tired of trying hard but failing miserably, you are ready to move from Romans 7 to Romans 8. You are ready to hear the good news about the Holy Spirit. That's our focus in the next chapter.

Chapter 4 | Review

Sincere Christians can become sincerely frustrated. Romans 7 shows us this painful truth.

———

Finding freedom is frustrated by "the flesh."

———

"The flesh" refers to the leftovers from your old life—your old mindset and muscle memory.

———

The flesh is stronger than your good intentions and best efforts to find freedom.

———

No condemnation? No kidding!

Romans 8:1–4

When you fall into sin again, in the very same area you've fallen down a hundred times before, how do you feel? If you are like me, you'd answer, "I feel guilty, lousy, stupid, discouraged and defeated."

Let me add one more word to the list: *condemned*.

I chose this word because it's the one Paul uses after telling us something of his own struggle with sin. In the previous chapter, we listened to Paul's lament about feeling defeated by sin. Even though he was a new person in Christ, even though he considered himself dead to sin and alive to God, he still found himself frustrated in his battle with sin. He wanted to do the right thing but kept doing the wrong thing. In his heart, he delighted to please God, but he found a civil war raging in his body. At the end of chapter 7, he cries out, "Wretched man that I am! Who will deliver me from this body of death?" (7:24). Paul was feeling condemned. Sentenced and stuck.

It's not a stretch to say most of us have felt—or currently feel— the same way.

But I've got some good news. Living with a heavy sense of frustration and condemnation doesn't have to be the end of the story.

It wasn't for Paul. It doesn't have to be for us either. I know that because Romans 8 follows Romans 7.

Romans 8 begins with good news for every Christian who has ever felt condemned by their repeated spiritual failures. Listen to what Paul writes in Romans 8:1: "There is therefore now no condemnation for those who are in Christ Jesus." You read that right: "no condemnation." Isn't that welcome news to a weary, worn-out heart?

Once again, you may have questions as you read Romans 8:1. You may wonder how Paul could move so quickly from feeling condemned in chapter 7 to declaring no condemnation in chapter 8. That's a good question. And we get a good answer in the first four verses of Romans 8. Read them carefully.

> ¹There is therefore now no condemnation for those who are in Christ Jesus. ²For the law of the Spirit of life has set you free in Christ Jesus from the law of sin and death. ³For God has done what the law, weakened by the flesh, could not do. By sending his own Son in the likeness of sinful flesh and for sin, he condemned sin in the flesh, ⁴in order that the righteous requirement of the law might be fulfilled in us, who walk not according to the flesh but according to the Spirit (8:1–4).

As we take a closer look at these amazing verses, we discover what Paul means when he declares "no condemnation" and why he can be so confident this is the case for every Christian. There are two key lessons we need to learn and the first one comes in verses 1–3.

1. If you are in Christ, you are not condemned to pay for your sins.

The announcement of no condemnation comes as big news since all of us have lived under God's condemnation. In the opening three chapters of Romans, Paul makes an air-tight case that no one stands innocent before God. Romans 3:23 indicts everyone who has ever lived: "For all have sinned and fall short of the glory of God." Romans 6:23 sentences us to death for our sin: "For the wages of sin is death, but the free gift of God is eternal life in Christ Jesus our Lord." Romans 7 piles on more condemnation by showing that even those who want to do the right thing continually come up short in doing it. No wonder we live under the weight of condemnation!

And yet, despite our repeated failures to obey God, Romans 8:1 declares, "There is therefore now no condemnation for those who are in Christ Jesus."

"Wait a second," you say, "I still feel a heavy sense of condemnation for my sin. When I mess up, my heart condemns me, other people condemn me and Satan condemns me as well. So, in my case, there is still great condemnation."

When we sin, we can feel condemned by our own hearts, by those around us and by Satan himself. And when others condemn us, they will often have solid evidence on their side. But they won't have God on their side. He declares "no condemnation" and his verdict is the one that matters. As Romans 8:2 explains, God has set us free from "the law of sin and death."

Again, you may ask, "But how can God set me free from condemnation when I sin? After all, God is just and righteous. Why doesn't he condemn me?"

The answer comes in verse 3: "For God has done what the law, weakened by the flesh, could not do. By sending his own Son in the likeness of sinful flesh and for sin, he condemned sin in the flesh."

Did you see the answer? The reason God doesn't condemn you for your sin is because *he already condemned Jesus for your sin*. God sent his Son Jesus "in the likeness of sinful flesh." In other words, Jesus took on our likeness, our humanity. Though he never sinned, he looked just like the rest of us sinners.[1] He was fully God (God's

---

[1] Robert Mounce writes: "If Christ had not taken on our nature, he could not have been one of us. On the other hand, had he become completely like us (i.e., had he sinned), he could not have become our Savior." Robert H. Mounce, *Romans*, New American Commentary, vol. 27, Logos online version.

Son) but also fully human (flesh and blood). What's more, verse 3 says God sent Jesus "for sin." Some translations read, "to be a sin offering."[2] Jesus came to sacrifice his life as an offering for our sins. For yours. For mine. For the sins of the entire world (1 John 2:2).

By dying on the cross "for sin," God "condemned sin in the flesh" (8:3). God condemned Jesus in your place. So, if you are "in Christ Jesus" (8:1), if you have united your life to Jesus through repentance and faith, you are no longer condemned. Jesus took your condemnation.[3] You are no longer condemned to pay for your sin.

You need to let this stunning truth sink in until you begin to feel the wonder of it and live in the reality of it. Most people—even Christians—have a hard time really accepting this truth. It seems too good to be true. We instinctively feel we need to *do* something to compensate for our condemnation. Our default response tells us we should help cover the costs of our repeated failures.

Back in 1986, a movie was released call *The Mission*. The storyline of the movie centres around Rodrigo Mendoza, a military officer turned slave trader. Mendoza is a vicious and violent man. In a fit of rage, he murders his own brother. Killing his brother almost kills him; he lives under a heavy weight of condemnation. So, he makes his way to a Jesuit mission, seeking absolution for his many sins.

The priest at the mission has him gather up the accoutrements of his old life—his swords, shields and body armour. After putting these weapons into a large net, the priests takes a rope and ties the net to Mendoza. He has Mendoza drag the heavy bundle to the base of a waterfall and then commands him to scale the cliff, from the base to the summit. We watch as Mendoza struggles to climb the steep cliff with the heavy net weighing him down. When he finally succeeds in making the arduous climb to the top, the priest cuts the

---

[2] See NIV and NASB translations.
[3] As Charles Cranfield writes, "for those who are in Christ Jesus . . . there is no divine condemnation, since the condemnation they deserve has already been fully borne for them by him." Charles E.B. Cranfield, *Romans 1–8*, International Critical Commentary Series (Edinburgh: T&T Clark, 1975), 373.

rope and we see Mendoza's heavy baggage fall to the river below.

It's powerful cinematography. But it's putrid theology. The message is that Mendoza, through his own struggle and striving, has atoned for his many sins. He's climbed his way from condemnation to redemption.

But the Bible is clear: *there is no mountain we can climb, no heroic effort we can make to cut us loose from the condemnation of our sinful baggage.*

The good news, announced in Romans 8:1–3, is we don't have to climb our way up to God. He sent Jesus down to us. More than that, Jesus bundled up your sins, my sins and the sins of the whole world, and carried them to the cross.[4] Jesus gave his life for our sins. God condemned our sins in the person of his Son. We are cut free from the baggage of sin and death, not because we are incredible, but because we are "in Christ." "There is therefore now no condemnation for those who are in Christ Jesus" (Romans 8:1). If you are in Christ, you are not condemned to pay for your sins. Jesus already did.

But the good news about no condemnation doesn't stop here. There's more in verse 4. In this verse you learn a second way you are freed from condemnation.

2. As you walk by the Spirit, you are not condemned to live in your sins.

Take a close look the wording of Romans 8:4: "in order that the righteous requirement of the law might be fulfilled in us, who walk not according to the flesh but according to the Spirit." You'll notice verse 4 begins with the words "in order that." This phrase signals Paul is about to give us the *reason* God condemned our sins in the body of his Son, Jesus. The reason was not only so you would be forgiven of your sins. God wanted more. He also wanted you to be

---

[4] See 1 John 2:2: "He is the propitiation for our sins, and not for ours only but also for the sins of the whole world."

freed from them. Jesus died so you could finally live according to God's "righteous requirement" and obey his law.

God's purpose in sending Jesus wasn't just to clean up the mess we had all made; it was also to make it possible for us to live new lives that please him and obey his commands.

You see, the word condemned has two different, but related, meanings. The word can mean to be "sentenced" for your sins. But it can also mean to be "stuck" in your sins, condemned to be forever enslaved to sins that displease God and destroy you and others. The first meaning (sentenced) comes out in verse 3; the second nuance (stuck) is highlighted in verse 4. Jesus died so you would not be condemned to live in your sins but rather to live in a way that fulfils God's desire and demands. To put it in theological terms, *God's goal in your justification is your sanctification.*

What's the key to getting unstuck? Verse 4 tells you—it's walking "according to the Spirit" (8:4). As you walk by the Spirit, you will not remain stuck in your sin.

At this point, I need to give you a bit of a spoiler alert for Romans 8. This chapter focuses attention on how God's Spirit helps you lose your sinful baggage. The Holy Spirit was only mentioned one time in chapter 7, but the Spirit is referenced over twenty times in chapter 8. If 1 Corinthians 13 is the New Testament's "love chapter," Romans 8 could be called "the Holy Spirit chapter." Romans 8 explains how God's Spirit makes it possible for you to live out your new identity as Christians.

Before we go further in Romans 8, let me pause and trace Paul's flow of thought from Romans 6 through 8. It's important for you to follow the train of truth revealed in these chapters.

Romans 6 lays the foundation by declaring that when you unite your life to Jesus through faith in him, you die to the slavery side of sin. You no longer are enslaved to sin; instead, you are now alive to God.

Romans 7 explains why you still struggle to live out your new identity in Christ. You continue to carry leftovers from your old life before Christ. Paul calls these spiritual leftovers "the flesh"—the old mindset and muscle memory pulls you toward sin and away from God. As Paul laments, the flesh consistently overpowers your good intentions and best efforts to live for God. In spite being freed from the slavery side of sin, you can still feel like sin always wins.

Right when you are ready to echo Paul's cry of frustration in Romans 7:24 ("Wretched man that I am! Who will deliver me from this body of death?"), a ray of hope breaks through: "Thanks be to God through Jesus Christ our Lord!" (7:25). The sunrise of hope dawns as Romans 8 rises from the shadows of Romans 7. You are not condemned to be sentenced for your sin because Jesus has taken your condemnation on the cross (8:1–3). But there's more. You are not condemned to remain stuck in your sin because the Holy Spirit has come to walk you toward freedom (8:4). Throughout the rest of Romans 8, Paul unpacks what it means to walk according to the Spirit and lose your sinful baggage. You could sum it up by saying that finding freedom takes being "in Christ" and walking by the Spirit.

There is still much to discover in the remainder of Romans 8 about how to walk by the Spirit. We'll do that in the pages that follow. But let me close this chapter by giving you an illustration that helps me understand what walking by the Spirit looks like in daily living. Let me tell you a story Bill Lawrence told me about Grandma Little. (You'll remember Bill Lawrence from chapter 2.)

When Bill and his wife, Lynna, lived in California's Silicon Valley, they would often drive to a retirement home to visit Lynna's grandmother. They came to give her an outing by taking her to their home for the afternoon. When Bill and Lynna arrived, they usually found Grandma Little sitting in her rocking chair, dressed and ready to go. Bill says he and Grandma Little replayed the same conversation each week. Bill would say, "Good afternoon, Grandma Little. How are you doing today?" "Pretty good" was her standard answer. "Are you ready to go?" Bill would ask. "Yes, but not too fast," she'd reply.

Then Bill would lean down and offer Grandma Little his arm to help her stand. As they walked down the long hallway to the parking lot, Grandma Little would lean on Bill's arm to steady herself. Grandma Little walked by the strength of Bill Lawrence. She used her legs but still needed his strength.

Bill told us he often imagines the Holy Spirit having a conversation with him at the start of the day. The Spirit whispers, "How are you doing today, Bill?" "Pretty good," he replies. "Are you ready to go?" "Yes, but not too fast."

And then, Bill told us, he consciously and continually leans on the Holy Spirit as he steps into the day. Bill Lawrence walking by the strength of the Holy Spirit, leaning on God's Spirit for the power to walk in God's ways and fulfil his righteous requirements.

That's a helpful picture of what it means to walk by the Spirit. We are active, engaging our minds, mouths and bodies. But we are also dependent, leaning on the strength the Spirit provides to enable us to move forward spiritually. As we walk by the Spirit, we do so with dependence and joy. For we know that, even though we stumble at times, there is no condemnation for those who are in Christ Jesus.

Are you ready to start walking by the Spirit and losing some luggage? In the next chapter, you'll discover this journey starts in your head.

Chapter 5 | Review

As a Christian, you are not condemned to pay for your sins—Jesus paid for them.

———

As a Christian, you are not condemned to live in your sin—the Holy Spirit empowers you toward finding freedom.

———

Freedom in Christ takes continual walking by the Spirit (remember Grandma Little).

———

Minding your mind

Romans 8:5–8

As we move through Romans 8, we discover the spiritual dynamic for finding freedom is the Holy Spirit. "The righteous requirement of the law" (holiness) can be fulfiled in us as we walk "according to the Spirit." As Grandma Little walked by leaning on the strength of Bill Lawrence, so we walk through life by leaning on the strength of God's Spirit.

But what exactly does walking by the Spirit look like in daily life? In practical terms, how do we walk by the Spirit?

Paul begins to unpack the answer to this question in Romans 8:5–8. Where he starts may surprise you. He begins by addressing *the way you think*. Evidently, walking by the Spirit starts in your head! It starts by minding your mind.

> 5 For those who live according to the flesh set their minds on the things of the flesh, but those who live according to the Spirit set their minds on the things of the Spirit. 6 For to set the mind on the flesh is death, but to set the mind on the Spirit is life and peace. 7 For the mind that is set on the flesh is hostile to God, for it does not submit to God's law; indeed, it cannot. 8 Those who are in the flesh cannot please God.

If you look closely at these verses, you'll notice the word "mind" shows up five times in four verses. Paul makes a clear connection between walking by the Spirit and minding our minds. Let me highlight three truths about your mindset that you need to keep in mind.

1. Your old way of thinking doesn't fit the new you.

Verse 5 contrasts two mindsets, two ways of thinking: the old way of the flesh and the new way of the Spirit. The old way involves setting your minds on "the things of the flesh." This mindset was the default way of thinking you had from birth. But when you were born again, you became a new person in Christ. While you still carry leftovers from the flesh, you are no longer "in the flesh but in the Spirit" (8:9). You have a new identity as one alive to God (6:11). In light of this significant change in your identity, you need a corresponding change in your mindset. Your old way of thinking no longer fits the new you.

In your old way of thinking, you saw life with yourself at the very centre. As someone put it: "You are the 'U' in Universe." God got pushed to the edges or voted off your mental island. In fact, verse 7 says the old way of thinking remains "hostile to God," unwilling and unable to submit to him.[1]

Your old way of thinking could be called "stinkin' thinkin'." Sadly, it still comes quite naturally to us even after we come to Christ. When someone says something mean or critical, what comes to your mind right away? When someone else gets chosen for a position at work you wanted, what thoughts rush to the front? When you drive by a billboard and see a larger-than-life model seductively dressed, what thoughts immediately come to mind? When you win an award or accomplish a major goal, what thoughts

---

[1] Douglas Moo explains, "Without the Spirit's mind-set, found only through union with Christ (vv. 9–10), people can only order their lives in a way that is hostile to God and that will incur his wrath." Douglas Moo, *The Letter to the Romans*, The New International Commentary on the New Testament (Grand Rapids: Eerdmans, 2018), 510.

crowd their way into your head, polluting your rightful sense of relief and joy?

You get where I'm going with this. Whether it's anger, jealousy, lust or pride, stinkin' thinkin' comes easily and naturally to us. To make matters worse, stinkin' thinkin' is reinforced by the world around us. Our culture regularly tells us to promote ourselves, to keep ourselves at the centre of life.

But the Bible gives a different message. It tells you this old way of thinking doesn't fit the new you. Because you are now in Christ, you need a new mindset.

2. A new mindset takes setting your mind.

If you are going have a renewed mind, you will need to reset your mindset. As verse 5 says, you must set your mind on the things of the Spirit. God's Spirit enables you to change your thinking to match your new identity in Christ. The Spirit helps you mind your mind.

Some years ago, when Linda and I were in London, England, we travelled around the city on the London Underground—the underground railway system for the metropolis. As the train approached each station, we repeatedly heard the same announcement, "Mind the gap." That phrase was foreign to us as North Americans. But it wasn't hard to figure out. "Mind the gap" alerted passengers to pay attention to the "gap" between the train and the station platform as they stepped from the train to the platform. If you didn't, you would stumble and fall.

In Romans 8:5–8, Paul broadcasts an important announcement as you journey toward freedom from sin. The Spirit wants you to mind your mind. If you don't, you will stumble and fall. Walking by the Spirit involves heeding his repeated reminder to mind your mind.

Let's say you come home tired on a Friday night and start watching a Netflix movie. The plot quickly engages you, but the storyline heads in a direction that's far from wholesome. Suddenly, you hear the Spirit whisper, "Mind your mind."

Later that night, you head to bed but have trouble falling asleep. Your thoughts drift back to old wounds caused by a family member or a former friend. You rewind and replay scenes from the past that stir up new bitterness in your soul. Then you hear the Spirit's quiet announcement: "Mind your mind."

As you drive to work on Monday morning, you anxiously anticipate what's waiting for you when you arrive. Worry and fear begin to flood your heart. Then the Holy Spirit breaks into your thinking to say, "Mind your mind."

One of the ministries of the indwelling Holy Spirit is to remind you to mind your mind. The Spirit does his work, but you and I have an important role in the process as well. In fact, verse 5 speaks of setting our minds on the things of the Spirit. The Greek word Paul uses for "set their minds" carries the sense of your outlook and your intentional focus.[2] A spiritual mindset requires *actively* reset our thinking, rather than *passively* letting our mind wander to stinkin' thinkin'.

The best way I know to set my mind on the things of the Spirit is to saturate it with Scripture. After all, the Spirit of God inspired the Word of God (2 Peter 1:21). So, when we fill our minds with Scripture, we know we're setting our minds on what the Spirit wants.

When I was in high school, a conference speaker challenged me to read the Bible at least five minutes a day. By this time in life, I had already begun to carve out time in the mornings to fill my mind and heart with God's Word. But this challenge to read it every day captured my attention and catalyzed a decision. For the past four decades, I've started my days reading God's Word. What a difference its made! The cumulative effect of inputting Scripture has helped transform my thinking. Oh, I've not gotten rid of all stinkin' thinkin' yet, but I now have a data bank of truth in my mind.

---

[2] The Greek word *phroneō* can carry the idea of holding an opinion (your outlook or worldview) and giving careful consideration (your intentional focus). *A Greek-English Lexicon of the New Testament and Other Early Christian Literature*, 3rd ed., Logos online version.

If you are longing to lose your sinful baggage and find greater freedom from the sins that pull you down, you need to join me in filling your mind with Scripture. Make time each day to read the Bible.[3] Then go deeper by studying God's Word in a joyfully serious way. Get in a Bible study at your church. Audit an online course from a Bible school or seminary.[4] Take it a bit further by memorizing some key verses that relate to your areas of struggle. As Psalm 119:11 says, "I have stored up your word in my heart that I might not sin against you."

You may hear this and think, "I agree that I should invest more time in filling my mind with Scripture. But my life is so crazy busy, I can't afford to take the time to do this." My comeback would be: If you want to find freedom from sin, you can't afford *not* to do this. Reading, studying, memorizing and meditating on God's Word will bring a change in your thinking. As Paul says a bit later in Romans, you will be transformed by the renewal of your mind" (Romans 12:2).

3. A new mindset leads to a changed life.

The idea of transformation also comes out in Romans 8:6–8. Take a closer look at these verses:

> [6] For to set the mind on the flesh is death, but to set the mind on the Spirit is life and peace. [7] For the mind that is set on the flesh is hostile to God, for it does not submit to God's law; indeed, it cannot. [8] Those who are in the flesh cannot please God.

A new mindset will lead to positive changes in your life. You will start to see changes inside you as you experience more of God's "life

---

[3] For a variety of Bible reading plans visit You Version's website: https://www.bible.com/reading-plans.
[4] To explore Bible and theology classes you can take for credit or for audit, visit Heritage College and Seminary's website at discoverheritage.ca.

and peace" (verse 6). Then, you'll notice changes in your actions, as you increasingly submit to God and live in a way that pleases him (verses 7–8).

Let me tell you how I've seen setting my mind on God's Word bring welcome changes in my life. One of the verses I've memorized is Colossians 3:12: "Put on then, as God's chosen ones, holy and beloved, compassionate hearts, kindness, humility, meekness, and patience." God's Spirit has been using this verse to help me deal with some of my own stinkin' thinkin'.

When I get criticized, my natural fleshly response is either to become defensive or to feel defeated. If I see the criticism as unfair or untrue, I get defensive, immediately wanting to push back and argue my case. On the other hand, if the critique seems painfully accurate, my thoughts become self-condemning and defeatist.

As defensive or defeatist thoughts linger in my head, the Spirit of God has been reminding me to mind my mind. He prompts me to remember Colossians 3:12. This verse begins with an amazing declaration of how God sees us in Christ. We are "chosen by God, holy and beloved." Even when others critique me (rightly or wrongly), my standing in Christ doesn't change. Because of God's grace, I remain chosen, holy and beloved. I don't need to defend myself or berate myself; I can remind myself of what God says about me. In Christ, I am chosen, holy and beloved.

As I let God's Word crowd out my natural stinkin' thinkin', my soul moves in the direction of "life and peace" (Romans 8:7). I'm able to respond with a heart of compassion, in "kindness, humility, meekness, and patience." I am not crushed by the critique and less apt to try to verbally crush my critic.

A new and renewed mindset leads to a changed life! This has been not only my experience but that of many others. Let me tell you about one friend who saw dramatic changes in her life as her mindset changed.

Susan[5] came from a very broken background. Early family experiences left her with lingering internal scars. Even after becoming a Christian, old, dark thoughts crowded into her mind and led her to take damaging actions. She struggled with self-harm, regularly cutting herself in moments of deep pain.

Then Susan volunteered to be a listener at her church's Awana program. Each week she listened to children recite the verses they were memorizing. She decided to join them and started learning the verses along with the kids. Hiding God's Word in her heart began to change what was happening in her mind. She gained a new inner stability—life and peace. The self-harm receded. Her life was transformed by the renewing of her mind (Roman 12:2).

What Christians like Susan and myself have experienced, is available to you as you allow the Holy Spirit to help you reset your mindset.

Many years ago, I read a helpful book by John White called *The Fight*. In it, he recounts how God's Spirit used God's Word to change his life. I still find joy and inspiration in reading his words. Here's what John White wants you to know about the impact God's Word had on his thinking and personal stability.

> If I could write poetry about it I would. If I could sing through paper, I would flood your soul with the glorious melodies that express what I have found. I cannot exaggerate for there are no expressions majestic enough to tell of the glory I have seen or of the wonder of finding that I, a neurotic, unstable, middle-aged man, have my feet firmly planted in eternity and breathe the air of heaven. And all this has come to me through a careful study of Scripture.[6]

---

[5] Not her real name.
[6] John White, *The Fight* (Downers Grove: Inter-Varsity Press, 1978), 55.

If you want to find your way to freedom, you will need to walk by the Spirit. That will start in your head as the Spirit helps you to mind your mind. But it doesn't stop there. In the next chapter, we'll see how the changes that begin in your mind begin to impact what you do with your body.

> ### Chapter 6 | Review
>
> Finding freedom requires you to change your stinkin' thinkin'.
>
> ---
>
> You must learn to set your mind on what the Spirit desires for you.
>
> ---
>
> The best way to set your mind on the things of the Spirit is to saturate it with Scripture.
>
> ---
>
> A renewed mind takes time, so keep soaking your mind in God's Word.
>
> ---
>
> Changes in your thinking will lead to changes in your living; you will move toward greater freedom in Christ!
>
> ---

Physical spirituality

Romans 8:9–17

When it comes to living a life that pleases God, does your body help or hinder you? If you think about it for a bit, you'll probably answer, "Both."

Sometimes your body is a big help to your Christian life. Your mouth sings praises to the Lord and speaks encouraging words to your family. Your eyes help you read the Bible or notice the sadness on a friend's face. Your hands let you lend a helping hand to a next-door neighbour.

But you will also have to admit your body gets you in trouble. Your mouth says words that wound. Your eyes look at things that pollute your soul. Your hands reach out for things that don't belong to you.

In the last chapter, which focused on Romans 8:5–8, we learned walking by the Spirit starts in our heads. The Spirit of God prompts us to change our mindset. He helps us get rid of sinful baggage starting with our stinkin' thinkin'.

But while transformation begins in our heads, it doesn't stop there. The Spirit goes to work in our bodies as well. Genuine spirituality has a very physical side to it. That's what we discover as we continue our journey through Romans 8. In this chapter we'll focus on Romans 8:9–17 and see how the spiritual life gets very physical. We'll learn how the Holy Spirit empowers us so that our bodies—eyes, hands, mouth, feet—become more of a help and less of a hindrance in living for Christ.

Energizing obedience

Look at Romans 8:9–11.

> ⁹ You, however, are not in the flesh but in the Spirit, if in fact the Spirit of God dwells in you. Anyone who does not have the Spirit of Christ does not belong to him. ¹⁰ But if Christ is in you, although the body is dead because of sin, the Spirit is life because of righteousness. ¹¹ If the Spirit of him who raised Jesus from the dead dwells in you, he who raised Christ Jesus from the dead will also give life to your mortal bodies through his Spirit who dwells in you.

In these verses we're told the Holy Spirit energizes obedience in our bodies. Verse 9 reminds us we have a new life in Christ. We are no longer "in the flesh," though the flesh is still in us (remember Romans 7!). So, if you are united with Christ, you are now "in the Spirit." Like every Christian, you now have God's Spirit dwelling inside you. This is a fulfilment of the New Covenant promises spoken by Jeremiah and Ezekiel.[1] It's also a game changer when it comes to living out your new life in Christ. The Holy Spirit energizes your body for obeying the Lord.

As verse 10 acknowledges, you still live with some deadness in your body ("the body is dead because of sin"). You retain some sinful muscle memory from your old life before Christ. That's why

---

[1] See Jeremiah 31:31–34 and Ezekiel 36:22–28. While these New Covenant promises were made with "the house of Israel" (Ezekiel 36:22), Jesus extended the blessing to believers from every nation (Luke 22:19–20; 24:45–49).

your body becomes a hindrance to holiness at times. But now you have the indwelling Spirit of God to empower your Christian life. As verse 11 says, the Holy Spirit gives "life to your mortal bodies." He empowers you to obey the Lord and live according to his righteous requirements (8:4).

Imagine it's Tuesday morning and you wake up feeling groggy and lethargic. You don't feel like getting out of bed. You have no burning desire to open your Bible and spend a few minutes reading and praying. But since the Holy Spirit lives in you, you can breathe a prayer and ask for the Spirit's help to get you going.

It's now Wednesday night, the evening you normally serve in the youth ministry at your church. But tonight, you're worn out after a long day at work. The thought of spending the evening in ministry seems draining. But you can whisper a prayer, asking the Spirit of God to give you strength to show up and serve well.

Or it's Friday afternoon and you need to have a difficult conversation with a friend. Everything in you wants to duck and run. You think of a dozen reasons to postpone. But since God's Spirit lives in you, you can cry out for courage to face what you'd rather avoid.

Romans 8:9–11 tells you the Spirit can and will give life to your body when you feel lazy and lifeless. He can empower you to open the Scriptures, show up at church or speak up in a challenging conversation.

I suspect you can remember times when you were sluggish, and the Holy Spirit helped you get moving. When he empowered you to do the right thing even though it was the hard thing. When he gave you strength you didn't possess. The Spirit of God truly gives life to our bodies so we can live out God's will.

Executing sin

But there's more. The same Holy Spirit who gives *life* to your body also wants to put some things to *death* in your body. We discover that in verses 12–14.

¹² So then, brothers, we are debtors, not to the flesh, to live according to the flesh. ¹³ For if you live according to the flesh you will die, but if by the Spirit you put to death the deeds of the body, you will live. ¹⁴ For all who are led by the Spirit of God are sons of God (8:12–14).

The wording of verse 13 is rather stark, even grisly. Paul says the Spirit helps us "put to death the deeds of the body." That's strong language. The Bible calls us to kill sin, not just curb it. To take it out, not just tone it down. To eliminate sinful baggage, not just moderate it. As John Owen warned, "Be killing sin or it will be killing you."²

Verse 13 promises the Holy Spirit will help us execute sin in our bodies. The Greek verb translated "put to death" in verse 13 can mean "to kill" or "to hand over to be killed." For example, in Matthew 26:59 we read the Pharisees were "seeking false testimony against Jesus that they might put him to death." The Pharisees didn't actually have the authority to execute Jesus. So, they planned to hand Jesus over to the Romans, the ones with the legal power to crucify him. But Matthew still indicts the Pharisees as guilty of putting Jesus to death—they were implicated because they delivered Jesus to the Romans.

When it comes to executing sin, you've probably discovered you don't have the power to kill it on your own. As we saw in Romans 7, the flesh is stronger than your willpower and best efforts. But the Holy Spirit is stronger than sin and the flesh. You can partner with the Holy Spirit in executing sin in your body. Your part is to hand your sin over to the Spirit to be killed by his power.

Let's say you have a sinful tendency to speak rash, reckless words that wound like a sword (Proverbs 12:18). You've tried to control your tongue, but it remains a major struggle. Romans 8:13 tells you what to do. Hand your sin over to the Spirit to be put to death.

---

2 John Owen, *On the Mortification of Sin in Believers* in *The Works of John Owen* (Edinburgh: T&T Clark, 1862), 6:9.

"Lord," you pray, "I don't want my tongue to speak words that sin against you and scorch others. I offer my mouth to you and ask the Spirit to help put sinful words to death." You are partnering with the Spirit of God to put sin to death.

Or you battle with lustful looks and thoughts. Again, you come to God and ask the Spirit to help you put this sin to death. Rather than excusing sin, you ask the Spirit to execute it. "Lord," you cry, "I'm sick of polluting my mind and heart with lustful looks. I give you my eyes and my mind, asking for your Spirit's help to put this sin to death in my body."

Here's another important insight. The verb translated "put to death" is in the present tense. This means the action (putting sin to death) is an *ongoing, repeated action*. Handing sin over to the Spirit so it can be put to death will remain a regular part of your Christian life this side of heaven.[3] Dealing with sinful baggage stands as one of the main reasons God gave you his Spirit.

Knowing this should help you recalibrate your expectations of what it means to live a Spirit-led life. Sometimes we have the false idea a Spirit-filled life is marked by small struggles and easy victories. Romans 8:13 counters that fantasy. The spiritual life is a fight of faith (1 Timothy 6:12). The good news is you don't fight on your own. You can get help from other Christians who are in the fight with you (2 Timothy 2:22). Best of all, the Holy Spirit lives in you to help execute sin.

I've spoken with some who doubt their salvation because of their relentless struggle with sinful baggage. They think, *Surely, if I were genuinely a Christian, I wouldn't have such a battle going on in my soul.*

Romans 8 brings a much-needed word of relief: the very fact you fight sin with the Spirit's help indicates you have become a child of God. Notice Paul's words in verse 14: "For all who are led by the

---

[3] "Human activity in the process of sanctification is clearly necessary; but that activity is never apart from, nor finally distinct from, the activity of God's Spirit." Douglas Moo, *The Letter to the Romans*, The New International Commentary on the New Testament (Grand Rapids: Eerdmans, 2018), 518.

Spirit of God are sons of God." In Paul's flow of thought, this verse refers to the Spirit leading us to deal with sin in our lives. As we join the Spirit in executing sin, we give evidence we are truly God's children. As Bishop J.C. Ryle explained, "The child of God has two great marks about him.... He may be known by his inward warfare, as well as by his inward peace."[4]

Encouraging closeness

You may read this and think, *This sounds incredibly difficult and draining.* You're right. Putting sin to death is a messy business. That's why what Paul says next will be a great encouragement to you.

> [15] For you did not receive the spirit of slavery to fall back into fear, but you have received the Spirit of adoption as sons, by whom we cry, "Abba! Father!" [16] The Spirit himself bears witness with our spirit that we are children of God, [17] and if children, then heirs—heirs of God and fellow heirs with Christ, provided we suffer with him in order that we may also be glorified with him (8:15–17).

Following the discussion about executing sin, these words speak comfort and hope. They bring sweet relief to my soul. Paul reminds us that the same Spirit of God who helps us kill sin also moves us to come closer to God as our "Abba! Father!" *Abba* is a family word, one used by children. The Spirit of God prompts us to address the Almighty God as our Abba, Father.

Verse 16 explains how this happens: "The Spirit himself bears witness with our spirit that we are children of God." The Holy Spirit gives you the inner assurance that you are God's child. He resonates in your human spirit that you belong to God.

---

[4] Cited in J.I. Packer, *Faithfulness and Holiness: The Witness of J.C. Ryle* (Wheaton: Crossway, 2002), 163.

Physical spirituality

If you are a musician, you may be familiar with concept of sympathetic resonance. Here's how it works. If you go to a piano, open the lid and hold down the sustain pedal, and then sing a note into the cavity of the piano, something surprising happens. Even without touching one of the piano keys, you will faintly hear the piano make music. The pitch of the note you sang resonates with the string in the piano that's tuned to the same frequency. You sing a note and the piano answers back with sympathetic resonance.

I believe Romans 8:16 points to a kind of spiritual sympathetic resonance that occurs in the lives of Christians. God's indwelling Spirit sings his music into our souls and our human spirits resonate back. He sings, "Come close to the Father," and our spirits respond, "Abba, Father." He sings, "Come close," and we resonate, "I come."

What's most stunning to me is all this happens *in the middle of our struggle with sin*! Remember, in the context of Romans 8, Paul is focusing on the messy business of killing sinful thoughts (stinkin' thinkin'—8:5–8) and outlaw actions (8:12–14). Right in the middle of our fight with sin, the Spirit of God calls to us to come close to God as our Abba, Father. That's amazing to me!

Let me ask you, how close do you feel to God when you are fighting with sin? Most of us feel we should keep our distance from a holy God as we struggle with sin. We imagine God must view us as a big disappointment. We assume we should only come close to God after we get things cleaned up in our lives. But here we learn *the Spirit of God sings to our spirits in the middle of the battle*. He reminds us we belong to God even before everything gets cleared up. His music in our souls assures us we are still loved. He helps us draw close to the Father.

Are you struggling with sin, seeking to hand it over to be executed by the Spirit of God? Be encouraged to know this is a regular part of a healthy spiritual life. Even in the middle of the battle, keep listening for the Spirit's witness in your human spirit that you are loved by God. Even now, draw close to the Almighty God, your Abba, Father.

The closeness the Holy Spirit prompts you to enjoy with God the Father is especially sweet as you groan your way to glory. That's what we will discover in the next chapter.

Chapter 7 | Review

The Holy Spirit energizes and empowers your obedience.

———

The Holy Spirit enables you to execute sin and put it to death.

———

The Spirit-filled life is not a life of small struggles; it's a fight of faith.

———

Even as you battle with sin, the Holy Spirit assures you of God the Father's love.

———

Groaning toward glory

Romans 8:15–27

Ajith Fernando has a unique perspective on North American Christians. Ajith lives in Sri Lanka, but he's spent a good deal of time in the US and Canada. His life in Sri Lanka has come with significant challenges. As a Christian, he's in the minority; the country is 70 per cent Buddhist. He and his family have survived Sri Lanka's long and bloody civil war. Ajith knows a good deal about disruption and suffering.

I once heard Ajith make a telling comment about his Christian friends in North America. He noted most of us have enjoyed a relatively peaceful life. In fact, we've come to expect life to be good. As a result, Ajith says, we've developed *a theology of glory* but not *a theology of groaning*. We tend to focus on the heart-warming biblical promises related to blessing and glory. We often overlook the heart-rending biblical promises related to suffering and groaning.

Ajith has it right when he says Scripture gives us both a theology of glory and a theology of groaning. If you wonder about that, just read Romans 8.

For the past few chapters, we worked our way through Romans 8. We've seen how the Holy Spirit helps us lose our sinful baggage and walk toward freedom in Christ. Now, as we come to verses 15–27, we discover an important reminder: life in the Spirit will always be filled with glory and groaning. In these verses we find a theology of glory and a theology of groaning. Both are essential if we hope to keep walking by the Spirit. We need both to keep us pressing on in our journey to gain freedom from sinful baggage.

As you read through verses 15–27, pay attention to the references to glory and groaning (you might want to circle each occurrence of the words). Notice how both glory and groaning are linked to the work of the Holy Spirit in our lives.

> 15 For you did not receive the spirit of slavery to fall back into fear, but you have received the Spirit of adoption as sons, by whom we cry, "Abba! Father!" 16 The Spirit himself bears witness with our spirit that we are children of God, 17 and if children, then heirs—heirs of God and fellow heirs with Christ, provided we suffer with him in order that we may also be glorified with him.
>
> 18 For I consider that the sufferings of this present time are not worth comparing with the glory that is to be revealed to us. 19 For the creation waits with eager longing for the revealing of the sons of God. 20 For the creation was subjected to futility, not willingly, but because of him who subjected it, in hope 21 that the creation itself will be set free from its bondage to corruption and obtain the freedom of the glory of the children of God. 22 For we know that the whole creation has been groaning together in the pains of childbirth until now. 23 And not only the creation, but we ourselves, who have the firstfruits of the Spirit, groan inwardly as we wait eagerly for adoption as sons, the redemption of our bodies. 24 For in this hope we were saved. Now hope that is seen is not hope. For who hopes for what he sees? 25 But if we hope for what we do not see, we wait for it with patience.
>
> 26 Likewise the Spirit helps us in our weakness. For we do not know what to pray for as we ought, but the Spirit himself

intercedes for us with groanings too deep for words. ²⁷ And he who searches hearts knows what is the mind of the Spirit, because the Spirit intercedes for the saints according to the will of God.

Let's consider what these verses teach us about a theology of glory and a theology of groaning.

1. The Holy Spirit assures us of our future glory.

In verse 15, Paul says we received God's Holy Spirit, whom he calls "the Spirit of adoption." Verse 16 explains the Holy Spirit bears witness with our human spirits that we belong in God's family. Since we are God's children, verse 17 announces, we get in on the family inheritance. As "fellow heirs with Christ," we will one day be "glorified with him."

You may read these words and wonder what's included in our inheritance. Paul answers your question in verse 23. He says our inheritance includes "the redemption of our bodies." This is part of what Paul means when he says we will "be glorified with him" (v. 17). When Christ returns in glory, our bodies will be resurrected and glorified with him. Paul celebrates this promise in Philippians 3:20–21,

> ²⁰ But our citizenship is in heaven, and from it we await a Savior, the Lord Jesus Christ, ²¹ who will transform our lowly body to be like his glorious body, by the power that enables him even to subject all things to himself.

If you belong to Christ, when Jesus returns, you get a glorious, resurrected body like his resurrected body. How's that for an amazing inheritance?

The Bible presents a high view of the physical body. Greek culture saw the physical body as a problem; they viewed it as a shell for the soul and wanted to discard it. In contrast, the Bible teaches that God created our bodies as a part of his good creation. In the new heavens and earth, we will live in resurrected, glorified bodies.

The promise of a new body makes your future glorious. Think of it. You will receive a body forever free from sickness. No more cancer, Crohn's disease, Alzheimer's or strokes. As Revelation 21:4 promises: "Death shall be no more, neither shall there be mourning, nor crying, nor pain anymore, for the former things have passed away."

But the best thing about your new body will not just be freedom from sickness. It will be freedom from sin. No longer will you need to put sin to death in your body. In fact, you will never struggle with sin again. You will be *finally, fully and forever* free from sin.

Because our inheritance is still coming, we must "wait for it with patience" (8:25). We should live with an expectation of being free from sickness and sin. And as we wait with patience, we find ourselves groaning in anticipation and longing. That's what we are told in Romans 8:15–27. Here's where we come to a theology of groaning. We also see the Holy Spirit at work in our lives.

2. The Holy Spirit helps us in our present groanings.

We are headed for glory but right now we live with a lot of groaning. Even the creation around us groans.

> [20] For the creation was subjected to futility, not willingly, but because of him who subjected it, in hope [21] that the creation itself will be set free from its bondage to corruption and obtain the freedom of the glory of the children of God. [22] For we know that the whole creation has been groaning together in the pains of childbirth until now (8:20–22).

Paul doesn't mean creation isn't good or glorious. Look around you and you'll see our world sparkles and shines with beauty. One summer, Linda and I made a coast-to-coast road trip to visit our families. Along the way, we drove through thick woodlands and open prairies. We climbed up the Rocky Mountains and drove along the rugged coastline of the Pacific Ocean. The beauty we saw was breathtaking. Yet, from what we read in Romans 8, we didn't see the creation in full glory. In fact, none of us have ever seen the creation as it was meant to look. Ever since our first parents rebelled against God, creation has been "subjected to futility" and in "bondage to corruption." The whole creation is groaning, like a woman in late stages of labour. It's longing to be reborn and remade into a new heavens and earth (see Revelation 21:1).

It's not just the creation that groans, verse 23 makes it clear we groan too. "And not only the creation, but we ourselves, who have the firstfruits of the Spirit, groan inwardly as we wait eagerly for adoption as sons, the redemption of our bodies." The Greek word translated "groan" means to "sigh." The same word shows up in Mark 7:34 where Jesus, after seeing the suffering of a blind man, is said to look up toward heaven and sigh. You sense Jesus' sadness at the ravages of illness that mar all creation, including humanity.

Paul says we groan as we wait for the "redemption of our bodies" (8:23). Anyone who has battled a long-term illness or disability knows this kind of groaning. When I pastored a church in California, I would visit Hank, a man in our congregation who had struggled for decades with a defective heart. Hank found it hard to breathe and difficult to get a good night's sleep. Sometimes we would talk about heaven and the resurrection body that awaited him. As I would pray, asking God to give him grace as he waited, Hank would whisper, "Yes, Lord." He was groaning toward glory.

While we groan because we get weary of pain, illness and aging, in the flow of Paul's thought, sickness is not the main reason for our groaning. Here in Romans 8, Paul's focus centres on our struggle with indwelling sin. We groan as we wait for freedom from the sin that lives within our flesh (7:24). We groan as we grow weary from putting sin to death in our bodies (8:13). We groan as we anticipate inheriting a new body that will forever be free from sin and death.

Chris Rice captures this longing and groaning in a song he wrote called "Prone to Wander." One line in the last verse says it well: "Freedom from myself will be / The sweetest rest I've ever known."[1] All of us who've grown tired of struggling with our own sinfulness, understand what he means.

As we wait for Christ to make all things new, all creation groans. All Christians groan. But that's not all. Verse 26 tells us the Holy Spirit groans with us.

> [26] Likewise the Spirit helps us in our weakness. For we do not know what to pray for as we ought, but the Spirit himself intercedes for us with groanings too deep for words.

On our uphill journey home to glory, God's Spirit empowers us to keep going as we "walk by the Spirit." The Holy Spirit also prays for us, interceding with "groanings too deep for words."[2]

I love Paul's honesty in verse 26. He admits our prayers often seem weak and feeble. "For we do not know what to pray for as we ought." Paul's right. Sometimes, as we face the complexities and complications in life, we find ourselves at a loss for words. We can't articulate the groanings in our hearts as we try to pour them out in prayer. But the Holy Spirit helps us; he joins our groaning and translates our unspoken longings into meaningful requests. He enables us to pray beyond our limitations.

Back in my university days, I attended a concert put on by singer-songwriter Alan Basham. For most of the concert he sat on a stool and performed songs on his guitar. Near the end of the evening, he

---

[1] Chris Rice, "Prone to Wander," in *Deep Enough to Dream* (Franklin: Rocketown Records, 1997).
[2] John Stott writes, "The Holy Spirit identifies with our groans, with the pain of the world and the church, and shares in the longing for the final freedom of both. We and he groan together." John R. Stott, *The Message of Romans* (Downers Grove: Inter-Varsity Press, 1994), 245.

moved to a piano and sang a very interesting song. The opening lyric said, "I've been told that I can't play piano." Listening to Alan play, it was clear he was singing the truth. He wasn't a pianist and could only plunk out basic chords as he sang. The next lines of the song explained why he was even trying.

> I've been told that I can't play piano.
> And it's true I don't play very well.
> But if I wait until it's perfect,
> Maybe I will never play at all.
> So, I'll play, play anyway.
> I'll lift my voice to heaven.
> I'll play, play anyway.
> I'll lift my voice to heaven.[3]

Something surprising happened as he continued to sing and pound out his basic chords. There was another piano on the other side of the stage. As Alan played, another man slipped to the second piano and began to play along. Only this second musician clearly knew how to play the piano. He filled in Alan's simple chords with beautiful runs and flourishes. Suddenly, the music went from simple to sublime.

Perhaps this pictures what Paul writes about in Romans 8:26. The Holy Spirit comes to help us as we groan and plunk out our feeble prayers. He groans with us and prays for us, bringing our weak, wooden prayers to God the Father in a way that transforms them into beautiful music.

So, on this journey toward glory, even as we groan, we will pray. Pray anyway. Because if we wait until we're perfect, we will never pray at all.

Romans 8 reminds us we need both a theology of glory and a theology of groaning. Knowing we are headed for a glorious future,

---

[3] Alan Basham, "Play Anyway," *Play Anyway* (Fullerton: NJC Records, 1977).

builds our anticipation and keeps us going forward. At the same time, knowing we will groan on the way to glory braces our expectations so we aren't derailed by difficulties along the way. Through it all, the Holy Spirit helps us lose our luggage and find freedom.[4]

If you wonder how to make sense of it all, you need to hear what Paul says next. In the following chapter, we come to one of the best-known and loved verses in the Bible. As we do, we'll discover what God is up to as we groan toward glory.

Chapter 8 | Review

Your Christian life will be marked by both groaning and glory!

You are headed for an eternally glorious inheritance—a resurrected body.

As you wait for your glorious inheritance, you can expect some groaning.

We groan to be free from sickness and from sin.

The Holy Spirit helps us in our groaning by groaning with us in prayer.

---

[4] "Paul encourages believers to endure temporary sufferings by giving them a glimpse of the beauty that awaits the children of God. The redemption they await is so stupendous that it will involve the entire created order." Thomas Schreiner, *Romans*, Baker Exegetical Commentary on the New Testament (Grand Rapids: Baker Academic, 2018), 431.

Up to something good!

Romans 8:28–30

There will be times in your life when you wonder what God is up to. Times when life gets puzzling or painful. When you feel you are losing the battle with losing your luggage. When you can't seem to win over sin. Times when life seems far more about groaning than glory. When you struggle to make sense of what's happened in your past or what's happening in your present.

When you wonder what God is up to in your life, make sure to turn to Romans 8. Because Paul answers your question in a clear, concise way. In Romans 8:28 Paul declares, "And we know that for those who love God all things work together for good, for those who are called according to his purpose."

Romans 8:28 tells you what God is up to in your life. He's up to something good!

Often, we treat Romans 8:28 as a stand-alone verse, extracted from the chapter in which it's found. But when we look at this verse in the context of Paul's flow of thought, we discover it carries special significance for all who long to lose their spiritual baggage and find their way to freedom in Christ. As we travel the trail toward glory, we can stay confident that God is always up to something good in our lives.

I realize this answer is rather generic. To say, "God is up to something good," still leaves us with unanswered questions. We wonder what good could possibly come from some of the things that happen to us. Thankfully, Paul gets down to specifics regarding what "something good" means in practical terms. If we look closely at Romans 8:28 and the next few verses, we discover three important truths which clarify the "good" God is up to in our lives as Christians. Let's consider them one at a time.

1. God is up to something good in your life— even when life isn't good.

You'll notice verse 28 says "all things" work together for good for those who love God. When Paul says, "all things" he literally means "all things." There's no footnote or fine print giving exceptions or exclusions to this statement. "All things" encompasses everything that happens in your life.

"All things" includes all the suffering you go through. Paul isn't saying all your suffering is good. He's saying God is up to something good in all your suffering. As Elizabeth Elliot used to say: "Suffering is never for nothing."[1]

"All things" also includes all the sins you commit, and all the sins others commit against you. Don't misunderstand. The Bible is not saying sin itself is good. It's never good. However, the Bible teaches God is always up to something good in the middle of human sin. You might remember the words Joseph spoke to his brothers after they had sold him as a slave. "As for you, you meant evil against me, but God meant it for good, to bring it about that many people should be kept alive, as they are today" (Genesis 50:20). Joseph doesn't rewrite history to excuse the evil his brothers committed against him. Instead, he understands God was at work in the middle of evil to bring about good purposes.

---

[1] Elizabeth Elliott, *Suffering Is Never for Nothing* (Nashville: B&H Books, 2019).

We may not always know the good God intends to bring out of our suffering or sin, but Paul says we can know that God is always up to something good in the middle of it.

Stop for a moment and let this truth sink in. The Bible is affirming that no matter what happens in your life—the good, the bad and the ugly—*God is always working for your good.*

The word translated "work together" is one you may recognize. The Greek word *sunergeo* gives us our English word "synergy." Look up synergy in a dictionary and you'll read "the interaction of elements that when combined produce a total effect that is greater than the sum of the individual elements."[2] In other words, synergy refers to something where the final product is greater and better than the sum of its parts.

I'm thinking of the chocolate cherry cake my wife, Linda, makes. The individual ingredients are not all delicious. Who wants to eat a tablespoon of baking soda or baking powder? Who enjoys a mouthful of flour or a half cup of canola oil? But when the various ingredients are combined by someone who knows what they are doing, the final product is mouth-wateringly delicious. A chocolate cherry cake is greater than the sum of its parts.

God knows what he's doing as he works in your life. And he has both the power and the wisdom to work all the ingredients of your life into something good. Even when life isn't good, God is up to something good. The outcome will be greater and better than the sum of the parts.

2. God is up to something good in your life— and it's to make you like Christ.

What is the good outcome God relentlessly works toward in your life? What "purpose" does he have for those who love him? (8:28) Verse 29 tells you: he wants you "to be conformed to the image of his Son."

---

[2] https://www.dictionary.com/browse/synergy; accessed December 15, 2021.

In other words, he's working to make you like Christ. He purposes to conform your character and transform your body so that you are both whole and holy. Your sinful baggage? Completely gone.

We've now come to the place in our study of Romans 6–8 where we get the big picture of the Christian's journey toward glory. Have you ever taken a hike up a mountain and come to a scenic overlook, a vista where you can look down and see the trail below? Romans 8:28–30 provides a spiritual overlook or vista for our lives as Christians. From these verses we can look back and get a panoramic view of where we've come on our journey toward holiness.

Looking back to where we started in Romans 6, you can now see your journey toward freedom started the moment you became united with Christ through faith in him. When you heard and believed the Good News of the gospel, your life was eternally linked to Jesus' life. God counted Jesus' death to sin as your death to sin. You died to the slavery side of sin. What's more, his resurrection became your resurrection to a new life. When you linked your life to Jesus by faith in him, your spiritual reality changed in an epic way. Now you must count yourself dead to sin and alive to God in Christ Jesus (6:1–11). You must see yourself as a slave to righteousness rather than a slave to sin. You can't live like you used to live because you're not who you used to be!

At this point, everything looked bright and promising. You had been set free to live out your new identity in Christ.

Then came Romans 7.

In Romans 7, you hit the headwinds of a harsh spiritual reality. While you died to the controlling power of sin, sin still lives in you. In Romans 7, Paul brings some bad news: You still carry leftovers from your old life—old ways of thinking and acting, which Paul calls "the flesh." As a result, you still struggle with stinkin' thinkin' and outlaw actions. In fact, Paul explains the flesh remains stronger than your good intentions and best efforts. Even when you want to do the right thing, you find yourself doing the opposite. How maddening and disheartening for a Christian who wants to please God!

Just when it seemed you were hopelessly stuck, unable to live in freedom and lose your luggage, you arrived at Romans 8. Here's where you learned the way to win over sin and find freedom in Christ: You must walk by the Spirit.

As you lean on the Spirit's empowerment, you find the power to live according to God's "righteous requirement" (8:4). Walking by the Spirit starts in your head and moves to your body—the Holy Spirit helps you change your mindset and execute your sinful actions. The process of transformation isn't automatic or easy. You still find yourself groaning as you grow. But in the middle of it all, God is up to something good. He working to conform you to the image of his Son, Jesus. He's working to combine all the ingredients of your life into something glorious.

In fact, verse 30 goes on to highlight the glorious outcome God is working to accomplish in your life.

3. God is up to something good in your life— and the end of your story will be glorious.

I want you to notice how verse 30 promises a glorious ending to your story: "And those whom he predestined he also called, and those whom he called he also justified, and those whom he justified he also glorified." All who are justified wind up glorified. In other words, those who are declared righteous ("justified") will one day be completely righteous ("glorified").

In verses 28–30, Paul gives you God's perspective on your spiritual life as a Christian. From God's vantage point, your story began before you did! Before your birth, God "foreknew" you. This means he set his sights and affections on you.[3] What's more, he also "predestined" you to be conformed to the image of his Son. Predestined

---

[3] Thomas Schreiner contends that, in this context, the term foreknew "highlights God's covenant love and affection for those whom he has chosen." Thomas Schreiner, *Romans*, Baker Exegetical Commentary on the New Testament (Grand Rapids: Baker Academic, 2018), 445.

speaks of a "prior destination" God has planned for you.[4] Prior to your birth, God purposed to bring you to a place where your life looked like Christ—in both character and body.

Next, God "called" you to himself (8:30). He worked in your life to bring you the gospel. He moved your heart to respond in faith. When you did, he "justified" you. Because your life was linked to Jesus by faith, God declared you righteous in his sight. I like how someone summarized justification: God treats me "just-as-if-I'd" never sinned.

Finally, verse 30 says God "glorified" you. This speaks of the glorious inheritance you receive in heaven—a person with no sinful baggage and a resurrected body like Christ's glorified body. This final stage of your journey is still in the future, but Paul talks about it as if it has already happened. You see, from God's perspective, it's as good as done! Everyone justified by faith will one day be glorified. If you are a Christian, you will make it to the end of your faith journey. And the ending will be glorious. God will finish the good work he has begun in you.

One of my favourite Christian musicians was Rich Mullins, an incredibly creative and insightful songwriter and singer. In addition to composing music, Rich was also an insightful writer. In one article, he wrote about an attic he remodelled into an apartment. The renovation process got messy and exhausting. At one point, Rich saw a parallel between the remodelling of the attic and the renovating of his soul. He writes,

> Sometimes…late at night when I look over the piles of dust and drywall and knee-deep debris that remain during this reconstructive effort, I am strangely moved by the place, and I proclaim the Gospel to it softly. I say, "I know how it hurts

---

[4] Douglas Moo writes, "The 'destination' toward which believers have been set in motion is that we might 'be conformed to the image of [God's] Son.'" Douglas Moo, *The Letter to the Romans*, The New International Commentary on the New Testament (Grand Rapids: Eerdmans, 2018), 555.

to be torn up. I am often choked on the litter left by my own remodeling. I know what it's like to settle…into the despair of believing that you are wasted space…. I know the pain of wanting to be changed and yet being distrustful of changes, of wanting to be worked on, but being suspicious of the intentions of the Worker. But here is some good news: "He who began a good work in you will carry it on to completion until the day of Christ Jesus." However messy it may be now, however confusing, and scary it appears, however endless the task may seem, we will someday be glorious, beautiful, alive![5]

In this spiritual remodelling project we call the Christian life, God is up to something good. And he promises to finish what he has started. The end of your story will be glorious, for you will be like Jesus.

Knowing how your story ends should keep you from letting up or giving up. Understanding that all who are justified will one day be glorified, should give you confidence that God is up to something good in your life. The end of your story will indeed be glorious. You will indeed lose your luggage. But there are some things you can never lose—as we'll see in the next (and final) chapter!

---

[5] Rich Mullins, *Attics and Temples*, http://www.kidbrothers.net/words/release-magazine/release-magazine-fal93.html. Accessed February 4, 2022.

Chapter 9 | Review

God is always up to something good in your life—
even when life doesn't seem good.

———

The good that God is up to in your life is to conform
you to the likeness of Christ.

———

You can be confident that God will finish the
good work he started in you.

———

Your journey to freedom has a glorious ending.

———

What you can never lose!

Romans 8:31–39

Sometimes you win by losing. That's certainly true when it comes to sinful baggage. To win against sin we need to lose our luggage. Victory involves getting rid of residual fleshly patterns that weigh us down or trip us up.

In Romans 6–8, God's Word leads us on a journey toward freedom in Christ by helping us understand and unload the sinful baggage we carry. As you begin to grasp the liberating truth of your identity in Christ and your release from slavery to sin, you gain hope that losing your luggage can actually happen. Then, as you learn to walk by the Spirit, what's possible becomes personal. You see changes in your thinking and behaviour. It's true that you still find yourself groaning as you grow, but you make headway toward holiness. The old luggage of sinful thought patterns and habits begin to lose their grip on you. Little by little, God conforms you into the image of his Son, Jesus.

While much of Romans 6–8 focuses on how you can lose sinful baggage, chapter 8 concludes by reminding you of what you can never lose. Romans 8:31–39 crescendos like the finalé of a grand symphony. In triumphant tones, Paul presents three glorious certainties you can count on, three unchanging truths to strengthen you on your journey through life. As we wrap up *Losing Your Luggage*, let's discover three things you can never lose.

1. God will be for you no matter who's against you.

The final 9 verses of chapter 8 are built around 7 questions. The first two questions come in rapid succession in verse 31: "What then shall we say to these things? If God is for us, who can be against us?" Paul essentially asks, "Since God has promised to work all things together for our good—since he is for us—who can possibly oppose us?"

Don't misunderstand. Paul doesn't mean we won't have enemies or face opposition. A few verses later, he mentions the painful realities of persecution, danger and death (8:35–36). Plus, he has already vividly described our ongoing fight with the flesh (7:14–25). So, when Paul asks, "Who can be against us?" he's really asking, "If God is for us, does it really matter who is against us?" God has committed himself to working all things together for your good. He has determined you will wind up looking like his Son. So, you don't have to worry about opponents or obstacles. Having God pulling for you trumps whoever and whatever pulls against you.

Someone may read verse 31 and think, *Paul, you're right. If God is for me, I'm in good shape. What worries me in verse 31 is that little word "if." What happens if God isn't really for me? Sometimes the way things go in my life, I wonder if he really is.*

Paul anticipates that question and answers it in verse 32: "He who did not spare his own Son but gave him up for us all, how will he not also with him graciously give us all things?" Do you get Paul's logic? He using what's called an *a fortiori* argument—the argument of the greater to the lesser. It works like this: If the greater of two related facts is true, the lesser one becomes even more certain. For example, if your friend promises to give you $100 dollars, she will certainly give you $20. If she's good for the greater amount, she will certainly come through with the lesser amount.

Can you see the *a fortiori* argument in verse 32? If God was willing to give us his Son to pay for our sins, he will certainly give us whatever else we need as Christians. This means you don't have to wonder if God is really for you. He proved that by giving his Son to die for your sins. He was "for you" in the biggest way possible, so you can stay convinced that God is for you today and forever. That's one thing you can never lose!

Even after reading verse 32, you may still struggle with lingering doubts about God being for you no matter what. What if you fail to measure up to his holy standards? What if you disappoint him one too many times? What if he eventually becomes disillusioned with you? Could he change his mind and turn against you?

Thankfully, you don't have to live with those questions unanswered. Verses 33–34 tell you what you need to know. In these verses we discover the second thing you can never lose.

2. God will acquit you when others accuse you.

Verse 33 begins with another probing question: "Who shall bring any charge against God's elect?" If you have a tender conscience, this question makes you squirm. After all, you're painfully aware of those who would happily accuse you of failing to live up to God's righteous requirements. There are people who could accuse you, pointing out specific areas where you've sinned. On top of that, Satan—the one called "the accuser"—makes ongoing accusations against you (see Revelation 12:10). And then there's your own heart! 1 John 3:20 speaks of our hearts condemning us. You know what it's like to have your own conscience pressing charges against you when you disobey or displease the Lord.

In each of these cases—when people, or Satan or our own hearts condemn us—they will often be right. They will have compelling evidence on their side. But they won't have God on their side.[1] I

---

[1] Thomas Schreiner explains, "The intent of the question is not to deny that some may lodge accusations against believers. Paul insists that no accusation will stick, since 'God is

know that because of what the Bible declares in Romans 8:33-34. Read these words slowly to let them breathe life into your soul: "Who shall bring any charge against God's elect? It is God who justifies. Who is to condemn? Christ Jesus is the one who died—more than that, who was raised—who is at the right hand of God, who indeed is interceding for us."

When anyone (including yourself) brings God an accusation against you, you can know this: *God himself justifies you.* The term "justifies" means to acquit or dismiss charges.[2] God, the righteous Judge, acquits you when others accuse you.[3]

"But wait!" one of your accuser's cries. "This can't be right. Ample evidence exists to prove this person sinned. It's a gross miscarriage of justice to withhold punishment!"

Verse 34 counters that accusation by declaring God didn't dismiss your sins without punishment. Your sins were fully paid for by "Jesus Christ who died." As we learned in Romans 6, when you trusted in Christ, God counted Christ's death as your death. You died with Christ; your old self was crucified with him (6:6). Your sins were fully paid for in Christ Jesus. At the cross, God showed himself both just and the justifier of the one who has faith in Jesus" (3:26).

But there's more good news in verse 34: "Christ Jesus is the one who died—more than that, who was raised—who is at the right hand of God, who indeed is interceding for us." Jesus currently[4] serves as your defense attorney when you are accused before God.

---

the one who justifies.'" Thomas Schreiner, *Romans*, Baker Exegetical Commentary on the New Testament (Grand Rapids: Baker Academic, 2018), 454.

2 The Greek term translated justifies (*dikaioun*) carries the sense of taking up a legal cause and rendering a favourable verdict. See *dikaiow* in *A Greek-English Lexicon of the New Testament and Other Early Christian Literature*, 3rd ed., Logos online version.

3 Thomas Schreiner comments, "In this context the forensic sense of *dikaoun* (*dikaioun*, to justify) is undeniable, since it serves as the antonym of *egkalein* (*enkalein*, to bring a charge). Schreiner, *Romans*, 454.

4 The Greek word for interceding (*entynchanei*) is in the present tense and indicates ongoing action.

He speaks to the Father on your behalf, declaring he paid for each and every one of your sins. No wonder Paul could confidently begin chapter 8 with the affirmation, "There is therefore now no condemnation for those who are in Christ Jesus" (8:1).

Knowing God justifies you because of the death of Christ gives you confidence of a second thing you can never lose: *God will acquit you when others accuse you.* This certainty frees you and propels you toward holiness.

I return here to John White's book, *The Fight*. His chapter on holiness has profoundly impacted my life. White's candid admission of his own spiritual struggle resonated deep within me.

> For many years I grappled with the problem of how I could live a holy life.... I read every book I could lay my hands on about "victorious living." Or I would feel that I had turned a major corner in my life and would seem finally to be in possession of the secret of sanctification. But I could no more hang on to the secret than capture a sunbeam in my pocket. [5]

He continued to describe the inward turmoil he faced as he failed.

> How could I confess the same sin for the hundredth time? Where was my sincerity? Having gone through "sanctifying experiences" several times, having dedicated my all to Christ, having rested in him, yielded to the Holy Spirit and trusted God to work in my life what I could never work in myself, my situation became hopeless.[6]

You get the sense that White felt crushed under weight of accusations from his own soul. Here's where the truth presented in Romans 6–8 came in to liberate him.

---

[5] John White, *The Fight* (Downers Grove: Inter-Varsity Press, 1978), 184.
[6] White, *The Fight*, 186.

Light began to break over me when I realized in the depths of my spirit that I was forgiven, cleansed, accepted, justified because of what Christ had done for me and not because of the depth of my yieldedness.... It was as though dawn broke. Suddenly the relief of knowing that I was forgiven and loved lifted the load off my spirit. I found that I was set free, free to be holy. To my astonishment I discovered that I wanted to live a holy life far more than I wanted to sin. Forgiveness freed me to do what I wanted most.[7]

White was liberated by the truth found in Romans 8:34. Jesus' death, resurrection and intercession are more than sufficient to cover the sins of each person who trusts in him. Because of what Jesus has done for you, you can have confidence that God will acquit you no matter who accuses you.

Paul's not done yet. Having given us two stabilizing, strengthening realities we can never lose, he provides one more in verses 35–39. And he saves the best for last.

3. God will love you when troubles attack you.

In verse 35, Paul asks two final questions, which focus on God's love for us: "Who shall separate us from the love of Christ? Shall tribulation, or distress, or persecution, or famine, or nakedness, or danger, or sword?"

Do you get what Paul is asking? He raises the issue of whether we can be certain of God's love when life gets brutal and turns painful. Can we still be sure that we haven't lost God's love when we lose everything else—health, security, safety, even life itself?

Paul has credibility to ask this question. I can't think of many people who lived through more hardship than Paul. If you read his autobiographical summary of the challenges he faced (see

---

[7] White, *The Fight*, 186.

2 Corinthians 11:23–30), you'll see he experienced all the traumas he lists in Romans 8:35.³ The man knew about hardships. Yet despite living in constant danger of losing his life, he remained confident that he would never lose God's love.

Most of us aren't so confident or resilient. Hard times take a toll on our bodies and souls, and also on our assurance of God's love. We feel ambushed, surprised the God who loves us doesn't shield us from tragedy and trauma. We forget Jesus' promise that trouble will certainly come our way (John 16:33) or Paul's matter-of-fact statement that "all who desire to live a godly life in Christ Jesus will be persecuted" (2 Timothy 3:12).

We take trouble as a referendum on God's love. Paul didn't. " No, in all these things we are more than conquerors through him who loved us" (8:37). How could he say that? How could he see himself as winning big when it seemed he was losing out? The reason: Paul was convinced he could never lose God's love. His confidence soars in verses 38–39:

> ³⁸ For I am sure that neither death nor life, nor angels nor rulers, nor things present nor things to come, nor powers, ³⁹ nor height nor depth, nor anything else in all creation, will be able to separate us from the love of God in Christ Jesus our Lord.

I love the realistic way Paul speaks of our life as Christians. Our struggle with sin remains real and relentless, even after we've been forgiven and given new life in Christ. We have been set free from sin's power to enslave us, but still feel its pull to entice us. We groan

---

8 Douglas Moo comments, "All these, then, Paul himself has experienced, and he has been able to prove for himself that they are quite incapable of interfering with his enjoyment of Christ's love. And the last—the 'sword,' death by execution—Paul was to find overcome for him in the love of Christ at the end of his life." Douglas Moo, *The Letter to the Romans*, The New International Commentary on the New Testament (Grand Rapids: Eerdmans, 2018), 565.

as we grow in Christlikeness. We find it hard to unload the sinful baggage we're carrying through life.

At the same time, we have great reason for hope and rejoicing. Through faith, we've been united with Christ Jesus in his death and resurrection. We died with him and have been raised to new life. His Spirit now lives inside us to empower our obedience. He works in us to renew our minds and remodel our behaviour. Little by little, he remakes us into the image of Christ, preparing us for a glorious future.

Chapter 10 | Review

God will be for you no matter who's against you.

God will acquit you when others accuse you.

God will still love you when troubles attack you.

You will lose your sinful luggage, but there are blessings you will never lose!

Conclusion

Joy in the journey

Most of the time, lost luggage is a bad thing. Usually, losing your luggage causes anxiety or anger. Plus, you often must work hard to get back what's been lost. That's not the case when the luggage you lose is unwanted, sinful baggage. Losing this kind of luggage brings relief and joy.

As we've journeyed through this book, you've become more familiar with three chapters in the Bible that map out the pathway to freedom. I trust you've already seen positive changes in your life. As you continue to walk by the Spirit, you'll continue to lose sinful baggage and find greater freedom in Christ. Remember, you can't live like you used to live because you're not *who* you used to be!

Let me wrap up by suggesting some next steps you can take to keep moving forward on your journey toward freedom.

1. Regularly renew your mind by reading through Romans 6–8.

One of my seminary profs urged us to repeatedly teach and preach through Romans 6–8. He said people won't get it all the first (or second) time through. They need multiple exposures to the life-changing message contained in these chapters. So, you'll want to revisit these chapters time and time again.

2. Earnestly ask the Lord to make these truths come alive in your soul.

Don't settle with conceptually knowing the biblical truths found in Romans 6–8, pray to personally experience them. Ask God to help you come alive to these liberating realities. In fact, use the word "COME" to summarize what you've learned and shape what you pray. Ask God to help you:

- Count on your new identity in Christ;
- Offer yourself to God;
- Mind the things of the Spirit;
- Execute sin by the Spirit's power.

And as you *come* to the Lord for help, remember that nothing can separate you for his love for you in Christ Jesus!

3. Memorize key verses from these chapters.

Memorizing Scripture helps you internalize its truth. You might want to start with Romans 6:11–14 or 8:12–17. Or push yourself to memorize all of chapter 8.

4. Guide another friend through the truths you've been learning in Romans 6–8.

Invite a friend to work through this book with you. You'll not only help a friend grow spiritually, but you'll also deepen your own understanding and application of the process of losing sinful baggage.

Keep pressing on. Even though we all groan as we grow, as you walk by the Spirit there will be much joy in the journey.

Appendix 1

Your personal "Baggage Check"

The first stop on our journey toward freedom involves doing a personal "Baggage Check." You need to know what sinful baggage you are currently carrying with you on your journey through life.

In just a bit, you'll be asked to take inventory to see what sins weigh you down. I realize taking this inventory won't be encouraging. You may be tempted to skip it. But I want to encourage you to do it anyway. It will help you get specific about the luggage you want to lose.

Let me highlight how you got this sinful baggage in the first place. The Bible points to at least three ways we accumulate baggage in life. Here's a short summary of each.

1. From Adam

Some of the baggage we carry comes to us because we are sons and daughters of Adam. Romans 5:12 says when Adam sinned, all of his descendants were affected. We are all born spiritually weighed down. What that means in practical terms is we all have certain sinful tendencies we didn't choose.

2. From early years

Some of the baggage you picked up may have come to you from others. We are all influenced by childhood experiences. We pick up habits and patterns from our parents and other significant people in our lives. Where do you think Isaac learned to lie about his wife (compare Genesis 20:2 and Genesis 26:7–9)? Where did Jacob's sons learn to be so deceptive (compare Genesis 27:19 and 37:20)? Some of what we pick up from our families qualifies as treasures; some of it is just sinful baggage.

3. From our own choices

Much of the baggage we carry comes as a result of our own choices. Whenever we choose to go against God's will, we face consequences. The Bible says we reap what we sow (Galatians 6:7). In other words, we accumulate luggage when we sin. We develop damaging habit patterns that become hard to lose.

The good news is God wants to help you lose your luggage. It won't all disappear at once, but God is committed to helping you travel light and become like Christ (Romans 8:29).

As you read Romans 6–8 and work through the materials in this book, you'll learn how God makes it possible for you to lose the luggage you've been carrying. But, before you can lose it, you need to check it.

Doing a personal "Baggage Check"

Here's how to do your personal baggage check. Carefully and prayerfully, look over the list and identify the sinful baggage you carry at this point in your life. If you want to really do a thorough baggage check, ask a family member or close friend to fill out the form about you.

The luggage checklist is largely based on Romans 1 and Galatians 5. In these two chapters Paul catalogues some of the

Appendix 1 | Your personal "Baggage Check"

"works of the flesh" (Galatians 5:19). That's another way of talking about sinful baggage!

You'll notice three suitcases in front of each item on the list. That's to help you indicate how much baggage you carry in various areas. If you have an *occasional* problem in an area, check one bag (✔). If you have an *ongoing, regular* problem in that area, check two bags (✔ ✔). If you have a *big* problem, check all three bags (✔ ✔ ✔).

☐ ☐ ☐ **Self-centredness:** A life focused on pleasing yourself rather than glorifying God; a me-first attitude in life.

☐ ☐ ☐ **Sexual impurity:** A degrading of God's purposes for sexuality in thought or action.

☐ ☐ ☐ **Greed:** A selfish desire to acquire (money, possessions, things); a continual discontent with what you currently have.

☐ ☐ ☐ **Envy:** An unpleasant sensation when noticing the prosperity or success of another.

☐ ☐ ☐ **Murder:** Before you skip past this one, remember Jesus put anger in the murder category (Matthew 5:21–22). Do you have a quick and hot temper that flares up to scorch and damage others?

☐ ☐ ☐ **Strife:** A tendency to be contentious; quick to quarrel.

☐ ☐ ☐ **Deceit:** Intentionally misleading others; concealing the facts to cover the truth.

LOSING YOUR LUGGAGE

Malice: Bitterness that shows up in harsh, sarcastic words or cold, unkind actions.

Gossip: Passing along information about others that should be kept to yourself or disclosed only to those who are part of the solution.

Slander: Speaking against others to tear them down.

Boasting: Attempts to draw attention to yourself to gain approval or praise from others; an exalted estimation of yourself.

Disobedient to parents (for those still at home): A stubborn, resistant or defiant attitude toward parental authority.

Faithless: A lack of confidence in God, a disposition to worry or complain, a tendency to doubt God when life gets hard.

Heartless: A heart callous or insensitive to the needs and pains of others.

Ruthless: A determination to get your way even when it means hurting others.

Approving of evil: Vicariously supporting evil by approving what is disapproved of by God.

Witchcraft/Occult: Dabbling or diving into the dark side of spiritual power. Putting yourself in God's place.

Appendix 1 | Your personal "Baggage Check"

☐ ☐ ☐ **Hatred:** A settled, ongoing feeling of ill will toward someone.

☐ ☐ ☐ **Discord:** An inclination to cause or contribute to relational friction; a history of leaving behind a trail of broken relationships.

☐ ☐ ☐ **Factions:** A tendency to divide up into cliques that intentionally exclude people who don't fit in with your group.

☐ ☐ ☐ **Drunkenness:** Drinking to the point of being impaired—physically, emotionally, relationally or spiritually.

☐ ☐ ☐ Other luggage (not on this list)

☐ ☐ ☐ Other luggage (not on this list)

Choose the luggage you most want to lose

Now that you've done a baggage check, it's time to focus on the luggage you most need to lose. While your desire should be to lose it all—in fact, you won't have much success in losing some of your luggage until you want to lose it all—it's hard to focus on getting rid of all your sinful baggage at once. So prayerfully select one or two kinds of baggage you most want to lose.

The luggage I most want to lose:
1.

2.

Discover other titles from Heritage Seminary Press

Paul and His Christian Mission

By Michael Azad A.G. Haykin
Includes Study Guide

The mission of the apostle Paul is central to the New Testament, where it was vital in the establishment of the early church and spreading the gospel throughout the world of his day. This study provides a concise but rich view of Paul the man and Paul the missionary. At his conversion to Christ, Paul was given a clear mandate to bring the gospel to the Gentiles. Paul loved the church, and he was zealous to win the lost to Christ. He appreciated and cultivated co-labourers in the work of the gospel, as he depended on the power of the Holy Spirit.

Paul's experience challenges the reader. Study guide questions are provided to help reflect on and apply the things that are learned in this short, focused study of Paul's life.

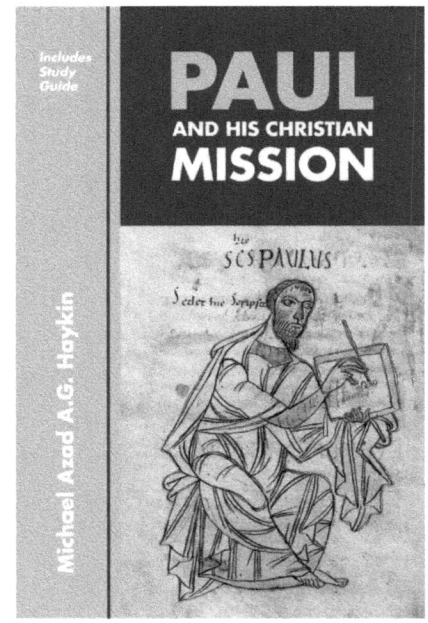

ISBN 978-1-77484-106-8 (Pbk)
ISBN 978-1-77484-107-5 (Ebook)
88 pages; 5.5 x 8.5"
Published December 2022

HERITAGE SEMINARY PRESS

An imprint of H&E Publishing
hesedandemet.com

Discover other titles from Heritage Seminary Press

This Poor Man Called: Stories and Songs of David

By David G. Barker
VOLUME 1 & VOLUME 2

David Barker takes a unique approach in this exploration of the psalms of David. Each chapter begins with a creative retelling of the biblical narrative, setting the scene for the psalm arising out of that experience. Having grounded the psalm in the "story," Barker then goes into a verse-by-verse exposition of the psalm, and provides some explanatory notes and a statement of the key message of the psalm.

At the end of each psalm exposition, Barker asks three basic questions: What do we learn about God? What do we learn about ourselves as the people of God? and What do we learn about the world? Answering these questions helps us to understand how David's experience shaped his theocentric and biblical worldview.

VOLUME 1
ISBN 978-1-77484-063-4 (Pbk)
ISBN 978-1-77484-064-1 (Ebook)
122 pages; 5.5 x 8.5"
Published Spring 2022

VOLUME 2
ISBN 978-1-77484-110-5 (Pbk)
ISBN 978-1-77484-111-2 (Ebook)
192 pages; 5.5 x 8.5"
Published February 2023

An imprint of H&E Publishing
hesedandemet.com

Dominus Deus fortitudo mea | The sovereign LORD is my strength

www.ingramcontent.com/pod-product-compliance
Lightning Source LLC
Chambersburg PA
CBHW042128100526
44587CB00026B/4218